IS THERE
STILL SEX
IN THE CITY?

Also by Candace Bushnell

Sex and the City

Four Blondes

Trading Up

Lipstick Jungle

One Fifth Avenue

The Carrie Diaries

Summer and the City

Killing Monica

Is There
Still Sex
in the City?

Candace Bushnell

Little, Brown

LITTLE, BROWN

First published in the United States in 2019 by Grove Atlantic
First published in Great Britain in 2019 by Little, Brown

1 3 5 7 9 10 8 6 4 2

A CIP catalogue record for this book is available from the British Library.

Hardback ISBN 978-1-4087-1179-8
Trade paperback ISBN 978-1-4087-1178-1

This book was set in 13.5-point Centaur MT by
Alpha Design & Composition of Pittsfield, NH
Printed and bound in Great Britain by Clays Ltd, Elcograf S.p.A.

Papers used by Little, Brown are from well-managed forests
and other responsible sources.

Little, Brown
An imprint of
Little, Brown Book Group
Carmelite House
50 Victoria Embankment
London EC4Y 0DZ

An Hachette UK Company
www.hachette.co.uk

www.littlebrown.co.uk

For JHC, the best MNB

Is There
Still Sex
in the City?

CHAPTER ONE

IS THERE STILL SEX IN THE CITY?

O NE OF the great things about middle age is that most
people become a tiny bit nicer and more forgiving.
That's because by the time you get to be middle-
aged, some real stuff has happened to you. You've learned
a few things. Like how a life that looks fine on the outside
can feel lousy on the inside. And how bad stuff is going to
happen to you, no matter how hard you try to be perfect.
But mostly how the things you thought were safe and sacred
suddenly aren't.

Like marriage. And love. And even the city itself.

My love affair with the city had started to unravel around
the time my dog dropped dead outside the mews near
Washington Square Park. A cocker spaniel killed him. Not
literally—technically it was an "accident." But it felt more
than coincidental: the afternoon before the sudden death,
I'd run into the killer cocker in the bank.

The dog had planted its feet and was growling. Embarrassed, the dog's minder—a young man in his early twenties with a face like a soft bun—reached down to pick it up. The dog then promptly bit him on the finger.

I shook my head. Some people are not suited for dog care and this kid was obviously one of them.

The next morning, I was up at seven thirty, priding myself on having made an early start to the day. I lived in a doorman building, so I'd often walk my dog without my keys or my cell phone, knowing I'd be back in two minutes.

That morning, when I turned the corner, I saw a small commotion at the other end of the block. Sure enough, it was the boy and the cocker.

I crossed to the other side of the street, smugly congratulating myself for having avoided that danger.

My dog took his time in the mews. In the meantime, the boy and the cocker had walked to the end of the block and crossed. The cocker spaniel was now on the same side of the street and in the next second came barreling toward us.

I saw it happen in close up: The frayed old black leather collar. The worn metal hasp attaching the leash to the collar. The dusty swirl of stiff leather particles as the hasp broke free and so did the dog.

The boy's muscles ignited and he stumbled after the dog, managing to tackle it in his arms just before it reached my dog.

I thought surely my dog was safe and that this was yet another canine sidewalk skirmish. The city was filled with fear biters; these incidents happened all the time.

I noticed that the leash in my hand had gone slack. I turned around to look for my dog. It took me a second to realize he was lying on his side on the sidewalk.

He was shaking. As I bent down, his eyes rolled back and his tongue—his great big dog tongue—slid out of the side of his open mouth.

Tucco, named after a character in *The Good, the Bad and the Ugly*, my husband's favorite movie, was dead.

My first instinct was to become hysterical. But I quickly realized that drawing all the attention to myself wouldn't be useful. A crowd had gathered and was offering to help, but no one knew what to do.

The dog, you see, was big. An Ibizan hound, he was twenty-nine inches at the shoulder and seventy-five pounds. About the size and shape of a small deer.

I wasn't sure I could lift him. And that wasn't the only problem. I had absolutely no idea what to do. I didn't have my wallet or my cell phone and my husband was, once again, out of town.

But then someone called the nearest vet's office and even though it wasn't open, they were sending someone there to meet me. The vet's office was several blocks away, and somebody hailed a taxi and somebody else picked up my dog and

3

the boy with the killer cocker spaniel said, "I'm sorry. I hope my dog didn't kill your dog."

He dug around in his pocket and extracted a crumpled twenty-dollar bill. It was dirty and worn. "For the taxi," he said as he pressed it into my hand.

I got into the taxi and someone placed the still-warm, dead dog on the seat next to me.

"Hurry, please," I said to the driver.

One of the things you learn about middle age is that life is not a movie. In a movie, the driver would have said, "Oh my god, poor you and your poor dog!" and rushed to the animal hospital and somehow the brilliant New York City veterinarians would have revived my dog and he would have lived. But in real life, the cab driver is not having any of it. He is not having your dead dog in the back seat of his taxi.

"No dogs allowed."

"It's an emergency."

"Why? Is the dog sick?"

"Yes. Yes. He's dying. Please sir. He may already be dead."

This was the wrong thing to say.

"He's dead? I can't have a dead dog in my taxi. For a dead dog you've got to call an ambulance."

"I don't have my cell phone," I screamed.

The driver tried to get me to get out of the cab, but I wasn't getting out and he wasn't going to touch the dog so eventually he gave in. He only had to travel three blocks up Sixth

Avenue, but the traffic was bumper-to-bumper. He verbally abused me all the way.

I tuned him out by reminding myself that no matter how bad my situation, there was another woman somewhere in the world who had it much worse. And besides, my dog dropping dead unexpectedly wasn't the most terrible thing that had happened to me lately.

The year before my mother had died. Hers was another unexpected death. When she was in her fifties—my age—she took hormone replacement pills. It was a standard prescription for a woman going through menopause. The problem was, the hormones could cause breast cancer, often deadly. And so, even though there was no history of breast cancer in our family and all the women on both sides of my family had lived well into their nineties, my mother passed away at seventy-two.

Back then I'd tried to pretend it was fine, even though it wasn't. My hair fell out and I couldn't eat.

It took me a long time to reconcile it. But my friends had been there for me. And so, too, had my husband.

When I arrived at the animal hospital, they kindly let me use their landline to call anyone I needed. Luckily I had a few numbers memorized. Like my husband's. I called him three times. No answer. It wasn't yet 9:00 a.m. He didn't start work for another thirty minutes. Where was he?

And my friend Marilyn. She arrived ten minutes later, speed walking from her apartment in Chelsea.

Marilyn hadn't had her coffee or a shower and like me, she was dressed in sweats. Our faces unwashed, our teeth unbrushed, and our hair uncombed, we looked at each other.

What now?

The dog died from an aneurism. That's what the vet thought, although she couldn't say for sure unless they sent the dog away for an autopsy. Did I want that? No, I didn't my friend Marilyn said.

My husband had always hated the dog. I wondered if the death of Tucco was a sign.

It was. I didn't know it then, but my relationship was like an aneurism—a death waiting to happen.

Three months later, in November, my husband asked for a divorce. He did it the day after one of those huge freak snowstorms. We were at my little house in Connecticut and there was no water or power. I couldn't imagine going back to the city with him, so I stayed in the country, scooping up snow and melting it over a fire to keep the toilet going.

The divorce wrangling began. It had the usual shockingly ugly moments but compared to other people's divorces, it was a relative breeze.

Except for one wrinkle.

The mortgage on the apartment. The old one had to be canceled and a new one drawn up in just my name.

I couldn't imagine it would be a problem, and neither could my banker. Especially since I had enough in the bank to pay for the mortgage anyway.

My banker kept reassuring me that it was going to be okay. Right up until the appointed day finally came three months later, when I walked into the bank and sat down.

I had a bad feeling. "Well?" I said.

"I'm sorry," he said. "It's the algorithm."

"I'm not going to get the mortgage, am I?"

"No," he whispered. And suddenly, I understood. I no longer checked off any of the right boxes.

I was (a) a woman, (b) single, (c) self-employed, and (d) over fifty.

And because I had no applicable boxes, I was no longer a demographic. Which meant, in the world of algorithms, I didn't exist.

I stood outside the bank in shock.

All the familiar landmarks were there—the glass-plate windows of the Knickerbocker through which one could see the old men in sweaters nursing their drinks at the bar. The deli where I went every morning next to the liquor store with the wound-up guy who talked nonstop about baseball. Like me, he'd been in the city for over thirty years.

I crossed the street and stared up at my building. I remembered how many times I'd passed this building when I first came to New York. I was going to NYU and Studio 54. I was nineteen years old and I'd already been published by a few of the underground newspapers that were flourishing in the city at that time.

I was so broke. But it didn't matter because everything was happening and it was all new and exciting. I'd pass the building with the white-gloved doormen in their gray uniforms and stop to admire the garden—an actual garden with flowers and tall grasses—and I'd think, Someday, if I make it, I'm going to live *here!*

Now I did live there. In a corner apartment on the top floor in the same building where, coincidentally, the actor who played Mr. Big also lived. The apartment had been featured on the cover of *Elle Decor*, and of all my accomplishments, it was the one my mother, a skilled decorator, had loved most of all.

And now I felt like the system had defeated me. Not only could I lose my home, but I was also about to become one more of the millions of middle-aged women who would get divorced that year. Who would have to get back out there, to once again look for a man who doesn't exist. And, like me, would likely have to find a new place to live.

I started to cry a little. But then I stopped because I realized I was too tired to cry.

I called Marilyn instead.

"Sweetie," I said.

"Yes," she said.

"I just wanted to let you know. I'm done."

With that, I left Manhattan.

✽ ✽ ✽

Unlike millions of other women who would get divorced that year, I was lucky to have made enough money on my own to save for the proverbial rainy day—of which, in middle age, there will be many. As a sort of fuck you to the bank, I paid off the mortgage, rented my apartment, hung up my high heels, and hightailed it to my teacup house in the hills of Litchfield County. And because there was plenty of room to run, I bought two standard poodles, Pepper and Prancer, and did what I'd always wanted to do ever since I was a little kid: I wrote whatever I wanted and I rode dressage horses.

Being what my father called a cocky son of a bitch, right away I got bucked off and broke a bone—after which I hobbled around with a walker and felt like an old person. I wasn't 100 percent sure that I should get back on the horse, but my father encouraged me. He reminded me of how I'd always "gotten back on the horse" as a child. Three months later, I entered a competition and won a couple of ribbons.

I woke up in the morning and inhaled the sound of silence.

I was happy.

I didn't think about my old life. I didn't think about New York. And most of all, I didn't think about men.

Nevertheless, six months into my retreat, I got a call from Tina Brown. She had a story idea for me. Now that the appropriate time had passed since my divorce, she suggested that I throw myself back into the dating world and write about what it was like to be dating over fifty. I could do internet dating. I could hire a matchmaker.

I cut her off.

I don't think so.

I wasn't ready to start dating. But most of all, I didn't want to. I'd been in relationships for nearly thirty-five years. I'd even experienced the full relationship cycle—fall in love, get married, and get divorced.

And now I was supposed to do it all over again? Was engaging in the relationship cycle the only thing I could do with my life? I thought about the time-honored definition of crazy: doing the same thing over and over again and hoping for a different result.

It was time to put an end to the cycle. And so I decided for the first time in thirty-four years to be man-free.

This also meant being sex-free. At this point in my life, I'm not a casual sex person.

I didn't talk about it, of course. The topic of sex—once the source of so much amusement, embarrassment, fear, and joy—rarely came up. My single friends had been single forever and not dating and therefore not getting any, while my married friends were married and dealing with kids and also—I imagined—not getting any. But every now and then, when I'd explain to some man that I wasn't interested in going on a date and frankly I might never be interested in going on a date ever again, he would gasp, "But what about sex?" as if I had just killed a kitten.

"What about it?"

"What do you do?"

"I don't *do* anything."

"But don't you *need* sex?"

"Do you? I've found that people who *need* sex tend to make bad decisions to get it. I've seen people blow up an entire world-class career just because they needed to get a little."

Besides, I had so much else to do that felt much more interesting. Like cooking elaborate meals. Learning Instagram. Making a pop song on GarageBand. My best friend was a girl called Angie. She lived up the road and she had just survived cancer and worked at a psychiatric institution teaching teenage kids Shakespeare. We would hike up and down the country roads, passing Calder's sculptures and Frank McCourt's house. There was no cell service up there, so we talked. About feminism and the meaning of life and the fever dream novels I was writing. We'd often stop by Arthur Miller's writing studio, the one he made himself with his own hands and where he wrote *The Crucible*. It was a small space, maybe eight by ten, with a smoothed piece of long wood attached to the wall as a desk. I'd go to the window and stare at the view of the woods and the dirt road and think: This is the very same view Arthur Miller must have looked at a million times. And how did he feel? Did he, too, despair of ever getting this writing thing right? And then I'd pray: Please, please let some of Arthur Miller's genius rub off on me.

Pleeeeasssse.

Well, it didn't.

During the time I spent in Connecticut, I wrote three books—every one of which my publishers hated, so much so that they refused to publish them. When I finally managed to get out a whole manuscript I thought they'd like, they sent it back with a black slash across every page.

Welcome to middle-age madness, where your career might possibly be over.

I called Marilyn. Help.

"Sweetie," she said. "I think you're going crazy up there all by yourself. Which is why the stuff you're writing is crazy, too."

And then my accountant called.

He, at least, had good news. If I sold my apartment, I could take advantage of a tax break. Paying off the mortgage three years earlier had been a smart move—the market had gone up, and with the one-time tax break I was able to make a profit.

Enough of a profit I realized, that if I was very clever and bought the cheapest real estate I could find, I could just afford a small one-bedroom in the city and a small, run-down house on the edge of a former fishing village in the Hamptons. A place in this hamlet was something I'd been hoping to secure ever since Marilyn moved out there two years ago.

Like me, she, too, had suddenly and inexplicably soured of the city.

Actually, that isn't true. Like me, she'd experienced a series of insults that made her feel like the city was trying to get rid of her as well.

Literally. The small family-owned building near the High Line where Marilyn rented for twelve years was going to be demolished to make way for an apartment tower.

Marilyn had no idea what to do. Then she lost a client who moved back to LA. And her dog needed a three-thousand-dollar operation.

It was the middle of winter and Marilyn couldn't stop talking about how it was so cold that if you went to the end of a pier and took your clothes off, you could freeze to death within twenty minutes. She said she'd looked it up on the internet.

This was alarming. Marilyn, who'd been taking Prozac for fifteen years, was one of the happiest people I knew. She talked to everyone and was one of those rare souls to whom you could safely confess your biggest fears without fear of being judged. And so at 8:00 a.m. on a cold morning in April, Marilyn went to see a shrink.

The shrink sent her home with some prescriptions that Marilyn filled at the drugstore. Then she went up to her apartment and promptly consumed an entire bottle of sleeping pills. I know, because I called her at 9:15 to see how the appointment had gone seconds after she'd consumed the last pill. She was barely awake but managed to answer the phone.

I called 911.

Thankfully she recovered, and it seemed like a good time for Marilyn to take a break from the city and regroup.

And so Marilyn headed out east to stay in a friend's cottage overlooking the bay in the Village. At first, she thought she'd stay a week or two. That turned into a month. Then two. It wasn't long before she became friends with a real estate agent who had the inside scoop on anything that might be affordable for a middle-aged single gal. Meaning properties with ancient appliances and peeling paint, the kinds of places developers wouldn't touch because there wasn't enough profit to be made.

Three months turned into a season and then a year, and it was winter again. And one morning, after Sassy had slipped on ice on her way back from Pilates and torn a muscle, she started complaining about how the city wasn't the same anymore and how great it would be if we all lived close by again. This gave Marilyn an idea. She was going to find us cheap houses and we were all going to live in the Village.

Years and years ago, Sassy, Marilyn, and I had lived on the same block and were always in and out of each other's apartments. And probably because we were fifteen years younger those times seemed exciting and happy, as successes built upon successes and one was quite sure that the future would take care of itself. Things changed, of course, but we always stayed close, and probably because we never had children or pressing familial obligations—Sassy's parents were dead and Marilyn's family was back in Australia—we still had holidays together.

Things don't usually work out as planned, but in this case, they did. With the help of the real estate agent Marilyn had befriended, both she and Sassy found houses and had taken up residence a few months before. Now, with my windfall, I would join them.

That spring I moved into a quaint run-down farmhouse about half a mile from Sassy and a mile and a half from Marilyn. At first it was just the three of us, but it wasn't long before Sassy ran into Queenie, whom we'd both known from our single days, and discovered she was living in the Village as well.

Back when we knew her in the city, she was a society it girl. But one weekend she came out to the Village to visit her mother, who was a famous artist and an even more famous grand doyenne. Eager to get out of the house, Queenie went to a bar, met a local guy, fell in love, got pregnant, and then after a brief, two-year attempt at staying married, got divorced. She'd lived in the Village since then and knew everyone.

Still, her boyfriend of the past ten years lived in another state and her daughter, now seventeen, had her own life, so soon Queenie joined in on our girls' evenings. This concept of being one of the girls was newish to her. She always said "the girls" as if with quotes, as if hanging out with other single women in your fifties was something that needed to be separated from her own life—with punctuation at least.

And then came Kitty.

Kitty was another mutual friend who, having landed her Mr. Big fifteen years ago, had happily disappeared into married bliss. Or so we thought. Now, as would turn out to be the case with so many of our friends, Kitty was all of a sudden getting divorced.

This was a shock. Kitty was my only friend who unreservedly believed in true love. All through her twenties and thirties she'd rejected men right and left because they weren't soul mate material. And then one day she walked into a neighborhood restaurant and sat down next to an older guy. They started talking. She went home with him that night, moved in with him the next day, and married him six months later.

Kitty and I lost touch for a while, but we reconnected while she was still married. I remember being struck by how in love she and her husband were. He told everyone that he couldn't live without Kitty and he'd rather spend time with Kitty than with anyone else.

I remember wishing that I, too, could have had a love like Kitty's, but knew it probably wasn't my fate. And I certainly didn't expect Kitty's marriage to end—or to end so abruptly—the way it did one Saturday afternoon when Kitty's husband came home unexpectedly early. He'd been playing golf and he was drunk, as was his golf buddy. Stumbling up to Kitty, he said, "You're a cunt" (he was English) and handed Kitty divorce papers.

Or tried to, anyway.

"Are you insane?" Kitty screamed at him. This wasn't the first time she'd seen him in this condition in the past few months; like most of the people in this story, he had issues. But the divorce papers were a new development.

Despite the fact that Kitty ripped them up, the papers were real. As was the airtight prenup. Which meant that Kitty had to move out and fast.

She rented a house in the Village so she, too, could be near her friends.

Kitty made it five.

"So what do you do out here?" Kitty asked one afternoon.

"Well, I write," I said.

"But what do you do at night?"

"I'm on a schedule. I exercise and take the poodles to the beach and then I have dinner early. Sometimes at four."

"At four?"

"I mean six," I said.

"By yourself?"

"Sometimes with Sassy and Marilyn. And Queenie."

"Dinner at six?" Kitty snorted. "That's no life."

She was right, of course.

And finally, Tilda Tia, who had been one of Kitty's married friends, magically appeared from the South of France. She'd just ended a twelve-year relationship with a Frenchman and was trying to start her life over again in the States.

And so we did what we'd done years ago, before there were husbands and children, demanding careers and all kinds of heartbreak: We gathered together to figure it out.

Specifically in the kitchen at Kitty's house.

And almost immediately, the way it had years ago when we were all single, the topic turned once again to sex.

"Where's the fun? Where's the excitement?" Kitty demanded.

"Where are the men?" Tilda Tia said.

And as I looked around at their eager little faces, I realized now might be a good time to find out.

And so, four years after I'd left, I returned to my old stomping grounds. As I crossed the bridge into Manhattan, now a middle-aged, single white woman driving a sensible SUV with two large standard poodles in the back, I had to ask the obvious question. Is there still sex in the city?

CHAPTER TWO

THE MONA LISA TREATMENT

I F THERE were any sex, I wouldn't be having it. Not according to my gynecologist anyway.

She was my first appointment upon my return to the city. This yearly visit is always terrifying, but it's something women like me have been trained to do: show your vagina to at least one person a year. Or else.

After the standard exam, she slid back on her stool and shook her head mournfully.

"Did you get that info I sent you about the Mona Lisa?" she asked.

"The Mona Lisa?" I felt the familiar trickle of fear. Had I missed something? Had I done something wrong? Was I now doomed?

I got dressed and headed into her office, bracing for the worst.

"Listen, sweetie," she said kindly. "The hormone ring isn't working. Your vagina is not *flexible enough*."

I made a garbled noise.

"When was the last time you had sex?" she asked.

Another garbled reply.

She rolled her eyes. I'd been seeing her for the last four years and every time she brought up sex I'd have to explain that I was "about to get around to it, very, very soon." Much like cleaning out the gutters.

But this time she wasn't buying it.

"That's why I brought up the Mona Lisa," she said, sounding like a woman in an advert. "It's a new laser treatment that restores thickness and elasticity to the vagina."

She slid a purple pamphlet toward me. "Think about it. You'll find it makes a huge difference when it comes to sex."

I coughed. "How much?"

"It's three treatments for three thousand dollars."

Three thousand dollars? No thanks.

Afterward, I went to lunch with a Hollywood producer. He wanted to discuss the possibility of some vague TV show that would vaguely be about sex and I was happy to be vague about it in exchange for an opportunity to put on proper clothing, go out to lunch, and eat with a cloth napkin.

"Have you ever heard of the Mona Lisa treatment?" I asked.

He went white.

He knew all about it. His wife—actually, his soon-to-be ex-wife—had undergone the treatment two years earlier, at fifty-two. At first, all had been fine, but then she told him he wasn't enough anymore and began an affair with the horse trainer he'd hired to teach his teenage girls. They were now getting married. This despite the fact that the horse trainer was over twenty years younger than the wife.

I had to feel sorry for the guy. He was nearly crying. He seemed shocked by the possibility that a younger man might prefer an older woman. I pointed out that if the roles were reversed—if it had been an older male who had run off with a younger female—he would have considered the age difference, and the behavior, normal.

Now, thanks to the Mona Lisa treatment, it seemed the shoe truly was on the other foot. If older women *could* have relationships like older men—meaning with partners decades younger than themselves—would they? Would more women give up their so-called age-appropriate men for younger, hotter guys?

Yes, they would, according to my friend Ess. Especially if, like Ess, they live in the I percent.

These are women who've spent years looking good for their husbands she explained. "After dieting, doing yoga, and spending thousands of dollars on Botox and filler, what's another laser treatment?" Indeed, it's not unusual for a husband to give his wife the Mona Lisa treatment for her fiftieth birthday.

Like most of these laser treatments, the Mona Lisa doesn't work for everyone. But when it does, watch out. Ess could name three women who had done it and had recently left their husbands.

The Viagra Effect

"It's like what happened when older men first got Viagra," she explained. "They suddenly had hard-ons and wanted to have sex with their wives and the wives didn't want to anymore and so the older guys left their wives for younger women. This is the reverse."

Sort of. The biggest problem with the analogy is that most women, unlike men, will *not* have the opportunity to experience this new dating phenomenon. As usual, there's a big difference in the price men pay for youth versus what it costs women.

How much will that "little blue pill" set you back? Not a lot, I'd wager. Like so many things male, it's probably covered by insurance. In any case, it doesn't cost anywhere near *three thousand dollars.*

Which made me realize that if I wanted to continue to explore this sex question, I was going to have to use what I already had: my bicycle.

Meet the New Bicycle Boys

Twenty-five years ago, when I'd first written about "bicycle boys," they were a rarified group. A little boyish, a little juvenile, they tended to be bookish and a touch nerdy and also annoying with their bikes, especially when they tried to bring them up to your apartment like they were some kind of pet. Their bike riding was considered a little silly and a little dangerous. It also signaled a lack of funds.

Today, the opposite is true. The bicycle boys are not only everywhere but like a virus that can't be stopped, they've mutated into dozens of different types.

Following are but a few:

The Family-Man Billionaire–Tech Guy

He has a passel of kids with different wives and somewhere on one of his thirty-million-dollar properties is a jungle gym. He likes to impress his other billionaire–tech guy friends with his prowess, so one of the things he does is road bike from New York City to Montauk—back *and* forth—in a day.

The good: He is rich, fit, and fertile.

The bad: He changes marriages the way other guys change bicycle tires.

The Pack-Rat

The pack-rat is a parallel-play type of man. He likes to ride in a pack with other men. He is usually not rich, but he is rich enough to spend two thousand dollars on a bicycle.

He is also rich enough to devote several hours a week to his "hobby," while his partner toils at home.

The good: He is trying to take care of himself, which means he will probably want to take care of other people, too—at least when he isn't riding.

The bad: He's the type who really pisses off his wife. She wasn't pissed at him at first, but now she is because they're both getting older and their kids are teenagers and he's out riding his fucking bike!

The Actual Bicycle Boy

This is a verifiable young person as opposed to a man who just acts like one. The actual bicycle boy may be shorter or smaller than you are, but he's a lot tougher and a much better rider.

The good: He can do wheelies.

The bad: You might end up trying a wheelie yourself and land in the hospital with a broken coccyx.

The Bachelor Boy

This is the guy on a weekend date with someone he met on a matchmaking app. The bachelor boy has only ridden a bike maybe three times in his life. On the other hand, since this is a guy who has seen *The Bachelor*, *The Bachelorette*, and probably *Bachelor in Paradise*, he knows that in the dating world of today, good guys must do things like ride bikes around quaintish summer towns. It's supposed to be fun but from the expression on his face, it clearly isn't.

The good: A part of him really is looking for "the one."

The bad: If you fall off your bike, he'll quickly replace you.

So is it worth getting on a bike to try to meet a guy? I went to Central Park to find out.

It was filled with people on bikes. The problem was that they all rode like they were in the Tour de France. Forget stopping one much less hooking up with one. And while there were plenty of Citi Bike people to explore, I didn't have the guts, the reflexes, or the stupidity to attempt to ride a two-wheeled vehicle in New York City traffic.

I decided to take the question out to the Village—and specifically to Tilda Tia.

Suddenly Samantha

Unlike me, Tilda Tia was open to any kind of dating experience. She'd been "good" for twelve years with her ex and was ready to be "bad" with her freedom.

Tilda Tia was Suddenly Samantha. She was also a maniac bike rider.

For the past week, she'd been texting about how she'd ridden fifteen, eighteen, and then twenty-one miles in under three hours and how we should aim to ride twenty-four miles in the same time or less. For some reason, I agreed. Even if we didn't meet anyone, at least we'd get exercise.

When I picked her up, Tilda Tia was wearing a peasant-style flowered dress and silver sandals like we were going to a beach party instead of on a twenty-mile bike ride. She had just had her hair done and refused to wear a helmet. Instead she stuck earbuds in her ears, as if these were going to save her.

I, on the other hand, was dressed for safety. I was wearing padded bike shorts and the neon-green safety vest Sassy had given me, along with a large helmet painted to resemble half a watermelon. My ride was an orange mountain bike that at one time had elicited admiring glances on the dirt tracks Angie and I used to ride in Connecticut.

It was exactly the wrong kind of bicycle to ride anywhere else. It was great for going over curbs and cutting across grass but too heavy to go very fast. At least not as fast as Tilda Tia.

I was fine until we reached the edge of the Village and hit the bike path. The first obstacle was a bridge. I'd crossed this bridge plenty of times in my car, never having realized how steep it was. Or how narrow the lane between the cars and the bikes was.

I made it halfway up before I wobbled and sensibly got off. I walked my bike over the crest to find Tilda Tia waiting impatiently on the other side. "You got off your bike?" she said. "We haven't even gone up one real hill."

"I'm afraid of heights," I said. I got back on the bike. At first, I pedaled furiously behind her, trying to keep up. When

I realized I couldn't, I slowed down and decided to do some research by taking note of my fellow riders.

You'd think biking would be a young person's hobby, but it's not. I quickly realized this as we passed one middle-aged person after another.

Like me, most were in okay shape. Meaning they were healthy enough to bike a few miles but not obsessed enough to hold the French fries later. Many were couples who, I assumed, had decided to get more exercise and were doing it together. In any case, they looked happy. Actually, that's kind of a lie. Sometimes either one or the other looked annoyed, like they couldn't believe their spouse had convinced them to do this and it had better be good for the marriage. But they were friendly. As I passed by, we'd exchange a little nod or wave in the style of old-fashioned boat etiquette.

Then there were the hard chargers. Also middle-aged men and women, they wore the latest gear and were mounted on road bikes with skinny tires and aerodynamic frames. They seemed to belong to some kind of club—a "super middle" one, as I would later discover—and they only acknowledged those who were just like them. As far as they were concerned, everyone else was just roadkill.

Finally, there were the friend pods. Mixed groups of men and women out for some bonding time. I could imagine the conversation that led to this event:

"Hey, let's get together."

"I'd love to, but I'm trying not to drink or eat too much."

"Me neither. Hmm, I've got an idea. Let's go for a bike ride."

"Yay!"

Tangled Up in a Pod

The friend pods were everywhere. It wasn't long before I was surrounded by one of them.

The problem with the pods is that everyone rides at slightly different speeds. Usually at speeds that are too fast to outbike and too slow to stay behind. The result is that everyone inadvertently ends up riding next to each other at close enough to the same speed to have to make conversation.

This isn't usually difficult or unpleasant. All you have to do is say something like "nice day for a ride" and kind of smile and nod and give a small finger waggle and eventually someone in the pod takes the lead and like ducklings the rest follow.

In this particular pod of four, that didn't happen. The woman and one of the men went ahead, but two men lingered behind. Sometimes this happens due to oncoming traffic that makes passing ill-advised.

The two men looked over at me, so I looked over at them. One was fairly nondescript. But the other one had a mustache. A gray-haired mustache that was paired with the jolly, largely line-free skin of a man who eats well and knows how to have a good time.

"Like your bike," he said with a smile.

"Thanks," I said, hoping they'd pass. They were trying to ride three across, which just isn't safe. I hate that. If a car hit one of us we could all topple like dominos.

"What kind of bike is it?" he said.

Really? Doesn't he know how dangerous it is to try to have a conversation between bikes when cars are roaring past at forty miles per hour? "It's a mountain bike," I said between gritted teeth.

And then, thank god, he nodded and he and his friend passed.

The next stop was the ferry. It took cars and bikers across the bay to an island that was known as a mecca for riding. The roads were picturesque and there wasn't a lot of traffic.

When I arrived at the dock, the ferry was just coming in. The friend pod was clustered by the side while Tilda Tia was right up at the edge of the dock as if angling to get on first. Which meant I had to pass the pod people to get to her.

"Headed to Shelter Island?" asked the mustachioed guy, as if Shelter Island weren't the only stop on the ferry.

I nodded.

"We're biking to the Ram's Head Inn for lunch. You should join."

"Thank you," I said, pleased. So far this bike-riding adventure was proving to be a good way to meet people.

I gestured at Tilda Tia and told him I was with someone.

He gave her the once-over, decided she was okay, and suggested that she come too.

"Success," I hissed as I wheeled my bike up to Tilda Tia. I pointed out the pod and told her they'd asked if we wanted to have lunch with them.

"No," she said.

"Why not?"

"Because they remind me of my first husband and his friends. And that's not what I'm looking for."

And to prove it, she wheeled her bike to the bow of the boat, putting as much distance between her and the pod people as possible.

Indeed, Tilda Tia had an entirely different type of guy in mind as I would discover ten miles later.

We were pedaling around a beautifully landscaped peninsula dotted with large historic houses when she suddenly pulled up short.

"There it is," she said, gesturing at a Victorian mansion. "My fantasy house. The house I'd live in if I had all the money in the world."

As we gazed at the house, our eye was drawn to a guy who came out of the house next door. He was dressed in a T-shirt and running shorts. He was perfectly muscled, with dark hair and an action-figure face. He was, maybe, thirty?

"Oh my god!" Tilda Tia said, as the guy reached the end of the driveway and began running. "It's the hot guy."

"Who?" I asked.

"Didn't I tell you about him? I spotted him two days ago by the harbor. He's the most beautiful man in the world." And she took off after him.

Please don't do this. Please don't make *me* do this, I prayed, as I pedaled hard to keep up with her. And because of this foolishness, it happened: I sustained an injury.

The streets in this very tony enclave were riddled with deterrents: speed bumps, small triangular obstacles, and randomly placed metal posts. As I was trying to avoid one of the posts, I hit a speed bump too hard and my feet flew off the pedals but not before one of them spun around and whacked me in the shin.

"Ow," I said.

I got off my bike. I was going to have a black and blue mark, and it hurt. At some point in the near future it would hopefully stop hurting, but in the meantime I still had to ride. At least far enough to find Tilda Tia.

She had disappeared over a small rise. I called her on her phone.

She answered immediately thanks to her Bluetooth headphones. "Where are you?" she said.

"I hit a speed bump."

"Are you okay? Do you want me to come back for you?"

No. I didn't. It wasn't that bad.

I caught up with her at the crossroads and showed her my leg.

I clearly didn't need an ambulance. On the other hand, we both decided that ice might be a good idea.

We headed to a popular beachside restaurant that was only, according to Tilda Tia's biking app, three miles away.

Fifteen minutes later, sweating and exhausted, we arrived. Once considered a hot spot, the restaurant was now filled with thirty- and fortysomething parents, complete with carloads of kids.

We sat down at a table and fanned our faces with the menu. "I can't understand why I'm so sweaty," Tilda Tia complained.

"I can," I said. I checked my phone. "It's only . . . eighty-nine degrees and seventy percent humidity."

This made us laugh. What the hell were we doing, two sweaty middle-aged women riding around in ninety-degree weather thinking we were going to meet men?

But no matter. It was nice in the restaurant with its multicolored rattan chairs and overhead fans. Outside the children played on the beach while the tourists pushed each other off a party boat anchored in the bay.

We ordered the house special, the Froze—rosé, fresh strawberries, and a splash of vodka whipped into a frozen confection. We ate French fries dipped in mayonnaise. Then, because it was that kind of day, we called an Uber.

CHAPTER THREE

THE TINDER EXPERIMENT

A FEW days later, having come up empty-handed during the bicycle-boy challenge, I was back in my apartment in the city when an email came in. A person named Emma wanted me to write a piece of experimental journalism about the dating app Tinder.

It was the word "experimental" that caught my attention. What did that mean I wondered.

I saw that Emma had included her telephone number. This meant the piece was important, because the phone was only supposed to be used for special occasions.

After a few email exchanges, we arranged a time to talk.

"Hello?" Emma the editor said. She explained that she was twenty-six and lived most of her life online. She confessed she wasn't very good at irl—in real life—and that the phone was very irl.

I asked what she meant by the word "experimental."

Emma lowered her voice. "I want you to tell us the truth about Tinder."

The truth? Was that the experimental part?

If so, the "truth" was that Emma worked for a magazine that celebrated sex and dating and mating and being a woman. And part of being a woman is being caught up in the industrial-romance complex where it's encouraged to believe in true love and romance and getting married and having babies and a far-off happy ending. This fantasy is sold in a million different ways, from reality TV to lingerie to nose-hair clippers. We buy romance and goddamn if it doesn't make us feel better.

Which meant chances were Emma wanted the same old, same old—a story about how online dating had its ups and downs but was mediated by a happy ending. Meaning someone gets married.

On the other hand, even I'd heard the rap about this notorious Tinder app, which wasn't even supposed to be for dating but for "hookups" only—a vague term that could indicate anything from lying next to each other on the bed watching Netflix to having down-and-dirty sex in a bathroom stall. It all sounded unpleasant: the guys were horrible, they sent dick pics, they never looked like their photos, they lied about everything, they'd hook up and never text you again. I'd been told the women were only judged on their looks and that guys would meet up with a woman and spend the whole time on their phones looking for other hookups. On and on it went, ending with: the guys only want blow jobs.

I don't think so.

"Please?" Emma begged.

"But why?" I said.

"Because," she lowered her voice. "I have friends . . . and Tinder is ruining their lives. And you've got to help them."

I wasn't sure I could. It had been a very long time since I'd done a piece of "journalism." But I still remembered one rule: Go in with an open mind. Don't decide what the story is before you write it.

"But what if Tinder turns out to be good? What if I like it?" I asked.

Emma emitted a short, harsh laugh and hung up.

I downloaded the Tinder app and clicked on the icon.

It's All About Money!

The first thing I realized is that while Tinder is ostensibly about sex, it's actually about money. In order to use Tinder, I immediately got snookered into agreeing to pay ninety-nine dollars a year for the rest of my life. That made me irritated. It meant when this damn Tinder experiment was over, I'd have to figure out a way to unsubscribe to Tinder, lest they keep charging me.

And then there was the Facebook link. I don't keep up with Facebook so by default it logged on to some ancient account and suddenly one of my photos appeared. Taken about ten years ago, of course. And there was my mini profile, which contained my first name and, yes, my age.

Already this was going wrong. Tinder is supposed to be a hookup app. Who wants to hook up with a fiftysomething-year-old?

Exactly two men, it seemed. Both of whom were smokers in their sixties.

This was not going to work. Being an old coot myself, I really didn't want to hook up with another old coot. What was new about that?

I examined my profile more closely and discovered that Tinder had automatically adjusted the settings for the age range of men it guessed I would be interested in. Meaning men aged fifty-five to seventy.

This made me angry as well. It was sexist for Tinder to assume that a middle-aged woman would only want to date what the app considered age-appropriate men.

To get even with Tinder, I reset my age range from twenty-two to thirty-eight.

Suddenly, everything changed. This age group was where the action was. Especially in the twenty-two to twenty-eight category.

I called up Kitty. "I can't even get through this swiping thing. Are you supposed to attract all these guys? Who knew so many young guys were interested in hooking up with women old enough to be their mother?"

And what the hell was I supposed to do next?

Naturally, no one my age had any damn clue. They knew no more than I did, except what I'd already heard: Tinder was a hookup app where women met guys, gave them blow jobs, and never saw them again.

The photographs of these prospective oral sex recipients were on playing cards, apparently underscoring the idea that this was nothing more than a game designed to keep users on the app for as long as possible.

I began hitting the Like button. Every time I did, some gimcrackery came up on top of my screen informing me that I had "matched." Yay. This was actually fun. It was even exciting. I was matching, whatever that meant.

A few seconds later, I understood. I could get messages.

I started reading them:

Do you have anything to do with "Sex and the City"?

Are you the Candace Bushnell?

What could I say? *Yes.*

Bing, I got back a reply:

You're too good for this app.

This was heartening. These men didn't know me, but they already had an idea about me. I was too good for this app. Yes. Yes, I was.

But this also made me nervous. If this app was so *bad,* why was everyone on it? And why were even the men who were on it saying it was bad? Shouldn't the men be saying it was *good* in order to get more action on it?

Perhaps these men on Tinder weren't terribly intelligent?

I got a very long message from a guy named Jude. It was all about how we had some Facebook friend Bobby in common and what a jerk the guy was and how he had a terrible hangover and it ended with something like: *Trying to date on an app when people know who you are must* sux.

Why yes, Jude, I thought. It potentially does sux. How considerate of you to consider my situation.

I wrote back to him: *Which Bobby?*

I looked at Jude's picture again. The one that had attracted me featured a shaggy, dark-haired guy with a beard and round glasses and a humorous, intelligent smile, as if he were somehow in on the joke that he looked like a very cute version of Snoopy. I scrolled quickly through the rest of his photos, including one of him playing drums. I saw he lived in Brooklyn and was in a band and was therefore, I assumed, out of my league.

But what did I know?

Champagne Dreams

And so, on a Wednesday night in my apartment, Emma and I organized a girls' roundup of Tinderellas—young women who were regularly on Tinder. The group, including Emma, ranged in age from twenty-two (the youngs) to thirty-three (the millennials).

Like most of the young women I meet, they were impressive. They were independent thinkers with a unique sense of style. Their careers were important to them and appeared to be a source of pleasure.

I poured champagne then passed around my phone. They immediately began analyzing the men who had matched with me.

"Oooh. Look at this guy. Emerson College. He's cute," cooed Hannah.

"I don't think I should go out with a college student," I said. "What about this guy who said I was too good for the app?"

A ruse, Elisa explained. "Guys always say you're too pretty or too good for Tinder. It's a line they use."

And as for Jude?

Everyone rolled their eyes. Apparently, his messages were too long. "On Tinder, guys either don't respond or they write you a novel."

"But if they're communicating, that's good, right?" I asked.

Apparently not, because when they do communicate: "All they talk about is themselves."

"Do you really think there's a guy out there who doesn't talk about himself or isn't obsessed with himself?" I asked.

A resounding no.

Marion had a question: "How do we as women navigate men's self-absorption? Or do we just have to accept it as fact and be happy if a guy pretends to pay attention to you for two seconds?"

Emma spoke up. She was the only one who not only had a *relationship* but was actually *married*. Emma explained it this way: "I feel like my husband is not at all self-absorbed, while I am. I only talk about myself and then sometimes I'll ask him how his day was. So it balances out. You have to be just as self-absorbed because it's every man for himself in a relationship. That way you can both care mostly about yourselves and then a little bit about the other person."

I laughed. "If that quote appeared ten years ago, people would say, 'These selfish bitches, *that's* why they're not with a man.'"

"But she *is* with a man," Elisa pointed out.

Aha, I thought. Here was a very good sign that some things had changed for the better. Women could speak their minds freely and men would still be happy to match with them.

But had Emma met her husband on Tinder?

No, she had not. And as more champagne was poured, everyone began dissing Tinder.

"Finding a guy on Tinder is about as much fun as trying to find an apartment," Gena said. "It's boring."

"All the guys on it in their twenties take prescription drugs and have been diagnosed by a shrink."

"They're like: 'The reason I can't text you back is because of ADD.'"

"Texting chemistry is huge because it's so rare," Corina said. "Texting with someone who's good at texting is hot. I love the slow burn."

"That would annoy the shit out of me," Gena interjected. "Someone matches with me and I say when can you meet in person? I'm not going to text forever. I think it's a young person thing."

"Like reaction gifs," Elisa said.

"Oh no. I *like* reaction gifs," said Corina, who was twenty-two.

"Gifs are a generational thing," Emma explained. "It's the same as when your grandmother doesn't know what an emoji is. I'm like: I don't understand a reaction gif."

But all this must lead to something good at the end, yes? Like a date?

"Dates?" Marion scoffed.

"I've had men take me to the ATM. That's an 'outing' to me," Corina said. "I'll tag along while they're running errands. I'll tag along while they're picking up dry cleaning."

"A guy once messaged me to meet him at a restaurant at eight p.m. I was excited. I thought, Here's a guy who actually can make a plan. But it turned out he only wanted to meet at the restaurant to pee, and then we went to a Starbucks where we didn't even get a coffee. And then we got kicked out," Hannah said.

Gena rolled her eyes. "The guy was probably crashing at his mom's house."

Being one of the olds, I had to ask the inevitable question: If dating is work and the guys are no good, why not try to meet people the old-fashioned way? In a bar?

Can We Talk?

"The problem with going to a bar is that you're not necessarily going to meet someone. I went to bars for years and I only met two guys that I've gone home with and slept with. Okay, maybe four," Gena said.

On the other hand, trying to find someone on a dating app has plenty of hurdles as well, especially when it comes to chemistry irl.

"There are so many guys I see online that I think: No, not cute enough, I'm not attracted, but if I met them in real life I *would* be attracted," Hannah said. "If you meet someone in real life you have a sense of their *humanity*. And online you don't have that."

The atmosphere suddenly became strangely tense, as if someone had said something politically incorrect.

There was a pause. "So you would prefer to meet people irl? If you could, *that's* how you would meet *everybody*?" Emma asked, as if such a thing were not possible.

"It's not that I feel online is bad," Hannah insisted. "It's just that the lack of context usually leads to disappointment. You can look at six good pictures of a boy and have no idea if you'll have any chemistry in person."

Or feelings.

"If you go into Tinder thinking, I just want to have sex, then you're fine. You feel like you're in control. But the second you have feelings it's a free-for-all," Corina said.

"'Catch feelings,' as the teens say," Emma added. "If you catch feelings for someone, you're done. It's the generation below us. It's getting worse for them."

"But I like having sex with someone and having feelings," Marion said.

"And if they have feelings for you, too, that's the best sex," Hannah said.

"Like, 'in love' kind of feelings?" I asked.

Nope. "We're talking about just a baseline level of caring about someone. Like I don't need you to meet my parents, I don't need you to be my emergency contact, just care *a little bit*," Corina said.

"Being nice is a winning quality in guys now. If you're *just not a psycho-killer* you're like the coolest," Emma said.

"Nice is also open and honest, but not 'I'm all about radical transparency.' If you can communicate and you're a six out of ten, I will definitely have sex with you," Hannah said.

"It doesn't take much. Just be a basic human being," Marion said.

Hannah turned to me and asked wistfully, "What were dates like when you were young?"

A Walk in the Park

Compared to what I'd been hearing for the past twenty minutes, dating thirty years ago was actually fun. Should I tell them about the helicopter rides? Or the long, romantic dinners at the Ritz in Paris? The yachts? The gondolas in Venice?

I looked around the room and felt queasy. Better keep it simple, I thought, pouring myself another glass of champagne.

"Well," I began cautiously. "Usually you'd meet a guy and you'd exchange numbers. And then you'd go your separate ways and a couple of days later he'd call you on your landline. You'd chat for a bit. It was really great if the guy was funny. And then he'd ask if you wanted to go out. And sometimes, if that first conversation was really good you'd end up talking for another hour. So by the time the actual date came around, you were pretty excited to see the guy. And the guy was excited to see you too—"

"But what did you do on the date?" Marion interrupted.

I took another swig of champagne. "You'd go to dinner. And you'd talk. You'd discuss things. And then after dinner, if it was a nice night or if it was snowing, you might go for a walk in the park."

"Oh my god," Emma gasped.

I was embarrassed. "I know," I groaned. "It's so *corny*."

"I don't think it's corny at all," Corina said. "To me, it sounds so appealing."

I laughed, wondering if I was being played. Was this nostalgia for the days of pre-app dating *real*?

Emma looked sternly around the room. "Everyone in our generation finds that kind of romance compelling, but at the same time it's just not realistic."

"I still like the idea of going for a walk with a guy, though," Corina said hopefully.

Hannah sighed. "I did that once and it stood out to me. As in, *look:* I met a boy and we went for a walk together in the park. It's the most romantic thing that's ever happened to me, ever."

Ten minutes later, I closed the door. Emma was right I thought, as I picked up the empty glasses. Tinder was bad. Just talking about it was depressing.

The next day, I braced myself as I clicked on my profile. And there they were: Those magical pink waves. Emanating from my face like I was a powerful princess in a Disney movie. I'd forgotten how comforting those waves were. And bingo! They worked! In two seconds I'd snared a man. A hot guy with muscles named Dave.

I liked him.

Keep playing? Tinder asked.

Damn straight.

It was like being in Vegas.

False Advertising

And then I couldn't stop playing. And talking about it.

I said, "No matter what everyone says, the truth about Tinder is that I've never had so many guys interested in me. In *ages*. And saying nice things. Like, 'You've got lovely eyes.'"

"So what if he's lying?" I'd continue. "No guy has said anything that nice to me in years."

And the women around me would agree, especially if they'd been married and were getting, or had just gotten, divorced.

They would gaze longingly at my Tinder matches. And then, with a sigh, they'd go back to emailing their bitter ex-husbands about the exchange of the teenagers for the weekend.

Out in the Village, Kitty and I looked over my prospects. It was like the old days when we were in our twenties and broke and would spend hours talking about men and trying to figure them out as if they were possibly the answer.

"You were always cute," she said. "But you never had this many guys interested in you before. Even when you were twenty-five."

"I know. And they're all younger. Something isn't right."

"Let me see your phone," she said.

She peered at my profile then laughed. "Well, no wonder. Those are the four best photos of you I've ever seen in my life."

"Photos?" I screamed. "What photos?"

I thought there was only the one.

I grabbed my phone.

Fucking Tinder. *What else had they got on me?* And how had they done it?

Kitty was right. There were *three* other photos on my profile, all taken back in the old days from some photo shoot where I'd had my hair and makeup done.

I knew the photos had come from my Facebook or Instagram pages but why those photos? Why only the younger ones? What was wrong with the older ones?

Most of my current photos reveal a smiling yet clearly middle-aged woman who looks like she could possibly be someone's suburban *mom*. Had a person—a Tinder *person*—actually chosen the youthful photographs or had some mysterious *sorting* program chosen the photographs that were the most mathematically attractive?

Had Tinder created a fake me?

This meant that before I'd even had my first Tinder date, I'd become a "false advertiser"—one of those people who make themselves out to be taller, better looking, bigger titted, richer, more glamorous, better traveled, better connected, more successful, and *younger* online than they actually are irl.

"What are you going to do now?" Kitty asked.

I groaned as we looked through my prospects. Richard, twenty-eight, was cute, but he also looked smug and judgy. Chris, twenty-five, was adorable and worked in the tech department at the *New York Times* but looked like he'd barely graduated from college. I swiped to Jude, thirty-one.

"What about him?" Kitty asked.

"He lives in Brooklyn. And he's in a band. He's sort of a cliché."

"So what? Maybe he'll take you to some cool clubs in Brooklyn. That would be good for you."

Choosing Jude

It was always going to be Jude I realized a few days later as I was getting ready to go on my one, and I hoped only, Tinder date.

I zipped up my dress, thinking about how, from the beginning, Jude had contradicted what others had said about men on Tinder. Starting with: "They can't make plans."

Wrong. Jude was a plan maker. It took only five or six or seven texts to arrange our "date"—a drink at a restaurant in Lincoln Square.

"The guys send dick shots."

Nope. Jude couldn't have been more respectful. After his initial hangover reference, his texts were polite and sober.

"The guy could turn out to be a psycho killer."

I'd been studying Jude's photographs for days looking for clues, and I was pretty sure I saw genuine kindness in his eyes.

Every person I'd shown his photo to agreed that he was definitely attractive and very much a "man-man," whatever that meant. On the other hand, the fact that he was attractive meant he was probably short. After all, you couldn't get good-looking, nice, *and* tall on your first spin around Tinder. And then I saw it: the dark hair, the beard, the glittery black eyes; if Jude turned out to be short, he would look exactly like Charles Manson.

Great.

A Tinder Unicorn

As I walked to the restaurant, I realized that Jude would be the very first person I'd ever met online. Even to me, it sounded impossible. How could that be when half of all marriages started online these days?

I immediately wondered if this Tinder date would become one of those kinds of stories: against all odds, two complete strangers meet on a dating app and end up being together. Nooooo.

I reminded myself that this encounter was pure research. I wasn't going to have sex with him, he was not going to become my boyfriend, and under no circumstances were we in any way going to be "together" in the near future.

I entered the restaurant and looked around.

I saw no one who bore even a passing resemblance to Jude, but what did I know?

Everyone had said that no one looked like their profile photos anyway.

I noticed some random guy in a dark shirt and trousers.

Could he be Jude? He didn't appear to be looking for anyone, but he wasn't going anywhere either. He was just standing there, sort of leaning up against the wall. Would Jude do that? Would he just *stand there?*

I went up to the guy. "Are you Jude?" I asked.

He looked at me like I was a piece of crud on the bottom of his shoe.

"No," he said sharply.

I backed off and went to the bar.

I took a seat next to a woman who was turned away from me. I ordered a white wine with a glass of ice on the side.

What if Jude didn't show up?

He would though. Of that, everyone had assured me. Because people on Tinder put so much work into arranging a meeting, they tended to honor the commitment. So there was that at least.

Then I suddenly sat straight up.

The woman on the other side of the woman next to me had begun talking. Loudly.

She was man bashing.

I scooted over a little on my stool.

All I can say is that I've heard a lot of man bashing in my life, but this was different. The vitriol, the bitterness, the rage. I hit the Record button and slid my phone closer.

She immediately stopped talking. I waited a moment, then slid my phone back. I looked at the recording and hit Delete.

"Excuse me?" she said in a loud, fake-sweet voice.

Uh-oh.

"I noticed that as soon as we started talking, you were doing something on your phone. And when we stopped talking, you took your phone back. Were you recording me?"

Shite. "I was," I admitted, coming up with a quick explanation about how I was doing a story about Tinder and just wanted to make sure my tape recorder was working.

"Tinder sucks," she roared. "It's the worst. I only go on it if I feel like getting a free drink out of a guy. And most of the time I can't even get that!"

I, on the other hand, apparently could, because Jude arrived at that very moment. And, well, let's just say that he was taller and a lot better looking irl than he was in his photos.

Had I just found a Tinder unicorn?

More Blow Jobs

Almost immediately, in what was now becoming a pattern, Jude started telling me how awful Tinder was and how the guys on it were only interested in one thing: sex.

"But what kind of sex?" I asked.

"Blow jobs," he said grimly.

"But what about cunnilingus?"

He shook his head. "Some women don't like it. Anyway, Tinder is all about the guy getting off. As quickly and as easily as possible."

"Surely all men aren't like that?"

He said nothing.

"Are you like that?"

He shook his shaggy head and ran his hand through his hair, embarrassed.

I decided that even if Jude had once been "like that," clearly he was trying to reform. That was probably why he'd agreed to meet with me in the first place.

Jude ordered a beer and immediately started telling me about his ex-girlfriend.

Of course, the whole relationship story was sad. It sounded like Jude really, really liked this girl. They were together for over a year, and she was the same age and he said she was a pretty big deal in the music business. She was successful he said.

But Jude had his own career. He'd spent the last three months touring with his band in Europe. Going to Berlin and places like that. Getting paid.

"I might want to move to Berlin," he said, glancing down shyly.

I'd had half a glass of wine by then and was feeling more relaxed. "You won't move to Berlin," I said reassuringly.

"Why not?" he asked.

"Because it's stupid. It's a waste of time. Far better to make what you've got here work." I almost patted his hand. "Don't worry. It will all be fine."

Or maybe it won't.

Jude revealed that his family was troubled. He thought his father was bipolar. His uncle had killed himself. Meanwhile, his grandmother insisted on ignoring it all.

"It's years of undiagnosed mental illness," he said, reminding me of my conversation with the Tinderellas.

Jude promised that he was okay and, perhaps feeling like he'd revealed too much, changed the topic to a recent trip he'd taken to Berlin. He listed a handful of drugs he'd consumed on a three-day bender. I was tempted to remind him that taking illegal drugs in a foreign country was almost always a really bad idea, but I didn't want to sound like his mother.

I gently steered the topic back to Tinder.

Jude pointed out that Tinder was gamed against women because it was created by the sexist minds of men who wanted to increase their chances of getting laid.

"It's all about what can you do for me? Men see women as commodities. Objects. Because it's on a *screen*," Jude explained. "That makes it not real. You can take that image of a woman and do whatever you want to her in your brain."

We talked about the male gaze and how awful it was. About how Tinder brought out the worst in guys, reducing them to nothing more than their base instincts.

The Ugly Truth

I woke up the next morning with what felt like an emotional hangover.

I felt bad about Jude I realized as I brushed my teeth.

This didn't make any sense. Why should I feel bad about *him*? After all, one was supposed to operate on Tinder without feelings, meaning one could assume the other person didn't have feelings either, so it didn't matter.

On the other hand, Jude had told me a whole bunch of stuff about his life and I was slightly worried for him. I knew I'd never see him again, but nonetheless, I wanted good things to happen to him because he was nice to me when he could have been a complete asshole.

And this, I realized, was the problem. I'd had a good experience on Tinder.

Valley of the Man Negs

So what was up with Jude's man negging I wondered.

I called my friend Sam. Sam, who was twenty-five, would tell me the truth.

"S'up," he said.

"Sam," I said. "Jude the Tinder date told me all this really terrible stuff about men." I gave him a quick recap. "You've been on Tinder," I added somewhat accusingly. "Is all of this true?"

"Ugh. Do you really want to go there?"

Thirty minutes later, Sam was pacing my apartment, clutching his man bun. "If there's one thing other men know, it's this: Men are stupid. They're run by their little heads. And there's a reason men call it their little head. Men consciously know that their penises should not be in charge. But they are."

"But why?"

"Because that's how it is when you're a guy today. You don't have a choice. You have hard-core pornography shoved under your face by the time you're twelve whether you want to see it or not. Same with Tinder. Even if you don't want to, you become addicted. If you're a guy like me, Tinder is designed to feed into the worst part of your psyche. The part that secretly wants to judge a beauty pageant."

"Really?"

"And that's why these guys can't stop swiping," he continued. "It's all about the numbers. Guys swipe left on every photo just to see what they can get. Plus, it's largely anonymous until you give your pictures life by saying something. And if the girl says something back, it's like she's already agreed to have sex with you. And so you just keep swiping. It turns you into a dog. A dog!" Sam gnashed his teeth. "When I think of my sisters . . ."

I thought back to what Marion had said about just wanting a guy to be "a basic human being."

"So you're saying all men on Tinder are assholes?"

"Not all men," Sam said. "Not me. But *most* men."

"What percentage?"

Sam shrugged guiltily. "Ninety percent?"

Was Tinder an app for people who hated themselves, I wondered? Was that why the men were so negative about each other? Tinder made them hate themselves and that made them automatically hate other men as well?

I'm Invisible

That evening, Sassy came into the city from the Village to meet up at what was supposedly a popular singles bar located in a hotel on Park Avenue. As I entered, I was taken aback. The bar was filled with attractive, age-appropriate men.

I joined Sassy at the bar. One guy in particular caught our eye: a handsome man with salt-and-pepper hair. Sassy and I decided to try to get the guy's attention the old-fashioned way: by catching his eye.

Fuck. We couldn't even catch the eye of the female bartender.

"Either we are old, or we've become invisible," I said, longing for a glass of white wine. "I know we're old," I groaned. "But we used to have *some* pull irl."

Sassy's friend Christie walked in. Christie was in her early forties, but like so many women in New York she looked about ten or fifteen years younger. She had dewy, perfect skin and lovely teeth.

Perhaps Christie, who was a never-married single, could put it together for us.

I said, "Christie, you're beautiful, you're young, and you're perfect. Is it us"—I gestured to Sassy and me—"or is it true that men no longer look at women in a bar?"

We're Commodities Now

Christie laughed nervously as she got the bartender's attention. "It's true. Guys don't look at you in a bar. You can't do that anymore. There's very little interaction in real life," she said as she ordered a round of white wine. "That's just the age we live in."

Sassy and I nodded. Clearly we didn't know the rules.

"I've done everything. I'm on every dating app. Tinder. Match. Plenty of Fish. Bumble. I even met with a matchmaker. You don't know what's going to work, so you have to keep planting the seeds."

Was she having any luck?

"I've met great guys, but the guys I like don't like me. Sometimes I feel like there's something wrong with me. If I could identify what it is, it might be easier to find someone."

She leaned in a little closer. "I think I need to sell myself more. Because no one is willing to buy me."

Sassy sipped thoughtfully on her drink. "Are you a commodity that needs to be bought?"

Christie nodded. "I am a commodity. And I need to repackage myself." She paused and looked around. "But doesn't everyone feel that way? Even if you're in a relationship with your friends you're a commodity."

"Look," she continued. "I love my life the way it is. I love my job, I love my friends. But I want that something extra. That's the only thing I feel like I'm missing out on. Maybe it's because I've never had that for myself, but I want that missing piece."

Keep Playing

As I sat down to write, I realized that as long as women still wanted men, and as long as there was still a chance to get one, even if the odds were gamed against them, women would keep playing.

I took the discussion to the young-youngs. Meaning they were too young to drink, too young to vote, and probably too young to be on dating apps like Tinder.

"As soon as I broke up with my boyfriend, I joined Tinder again because he'd made me delete my profile when I was with him," said the sixteen-year-old. "And immediately I started feeling good. All these people were liking my pictures."

"It's the attention. The attention makes you think everything in your life is great," said the seventeen-year-old. She leaned back in her chair and sipped her latte. "I always say this. All social media is like a drug. I know that every time I get a like on Instagram my body is flooded with endorphins."

"Listen." The sixteen-year-old looked me in the eye. "A lot of the time you have a hookup. And you're fine with it just being a hookup. You don't want anything more. But then the guy starts bothering you. And all you want to do is go back on Tinder. Because on Tinder, it's all about the chase."

Tinder Always Wins

Emma called me up. "What's the takeaway?" she asked.

The word "takeaway" made me uneasy. It made me think of fast-food restaurants and those giant menus lit up with photographs of mouthwatering food.

I wondered if *this* was the future of dating: *Takeaway*. People would become items to be ordered from a menu. Like a hamburger done *exactly your way*.

I was still pondering this when Jude texted me and asked if I wanted to see *Henry IV* at two o'clock at the Brooklyn Academy of Music on Saturday. He'd already purchased the tickets.

I couldn't say no.

And so, on a cold Saturday I got into a taxi and headed to Brooklyn.

The taxi ride was thirty dollars, but I didn't mind. Jude had paid for the tickets, and they probably cost a lot more than that. I reminded myself to split the ticket price with him.

I got to the theater and went inside.

And then, like the classic sad sack who's about to be stood up, I looked around at all the people. And as they eventually paired off, I realized Jude was not coming.

I texted him: *Hey, did we mess up? I'm at BAM.* And then, for reasons still unknown to me, I added: *Eeeee.*

I wasn't really expecting to hear from Jude again, but I did. That evening I got a text: *Oh fuck wow I had no idea how late it was. I am so, so sorry. I ended up in the ER last night.*

I sighed. Of course you did.

For a moment, I was curious about this so-called ER adventure. But the moment passed. And then I realized I, too, had become Tinderized. Because I just didn't care.

Apparently Jude did, though. The next day, I got another text:

Hey sorry for the rushed message. I just got home from the hospital and had no idea it was so late and had a ton of messages/voice mails . . . so so so so sorry for screwing up our plans! Totally understand if you're really pissed at me . . . I've been a mess. I was out last night and did too many drugs and got really drunk and apparently tried to get into someone's car thinking it was mine and the cops came and almost arrested me (I was handcuffed for a bit) and then sent me to the ER. I think they may have sedated me or something because I ended up unconscious for about 12 hours. Again, so sorry I was really looking forward to it and am pretty pissed at myself.

I texted him back: *Glad you're okay,* followed by a smiley face.

And then I laughed. I'd been brilliantly played by Tinder. Tinder is the house, and the house always wins.

The Russian Explains It All

I was outside, taking a break from a black-tie dinner at the Cipriani on Forty-Second Street when I noticed a woman standing on the steps between the columns of the old bank. She was tall and lean with masses of hair, dressed like a woman warrior in a second-skin cocktail dress and thigh-high wrapped leather boots.

I was gaping at her, of course. She saw me staring and came over.

"Got a light?" she asked with a Russian accent.

"Sure," I said.

We stood for a moment in silence, watching the I percent come and go in their town cars and SUVs.

"Tell me something," I said. "Are you on Tinder?"

"Of course," she laughed.

"But why? You're beautiful. You don't look like you need to go on Tinder."

She nodded in agreement and then beckoned me closer.

"You want to know the secret to Tinder?"

"Yes?"

"When you go on it you get lots more Instagram followers."

I stared at her. "Really? That's it? It's all about Instagram followers? But what about . . . all the women who are going on it to find relationships? And then they meet guys, but they don't get a second date? Or else the guy likes her, but she doesn't like him?"

The Russian turned. "*That?*" she asked. "You know the answer to *that*."

"No," I said. "I don't."

"It's because women never change. It's the same old story." She paused to flick away her cigarette. "We women don't know what we want!"

And with a laugh of triumph, she spun around and was gone.

For a moment, I just stood there. Was she right? Was it really as simple as that hoary old paternalistic cliché?

And then I realized she was wrong. Because women do know what they want. And mostly, it seems, what they want is simple. A modicum of respect. To be treated, as Hannah said, like a human being.

I held out my hand for an old-fashioned yellow taxi.

"Where to?" the driver asked.

I smiled.

Home.

CHAPTER FOUR

GET READY LADIES: THE CUBS ARE COMING TO TOWN

RECENTLY, OUT in the Village, Marilyn had a tangle with a twenty-one-year-old boy-cub. The guy came to her house to deliver some boxes, and apparently he was the friendly type, because he began chatting her up. After fifteen minutes, she finally managed to shoo him out of the house by reminding him for the sixth time that she had a conference call.

She did her call and forgot all about the delivery boy—until 6:00 p.m. when he texted her.

You're so beautiful, he wrote. *Can we hang out? Or is twenty-one too young for you?*

Yes, it is too young, she wrote back.

Immediately she got another text: *Ouch! That's harsh.*

We brushed the incident off as an anomaly, but two days later Sassy had a similar encounter. She went to hear an opera singer at a private party hosted by a society lady of a certain age. When the concert ended and all the middle-aged people hurried to their cars to get home in time for a good night's sleep, Sassy was approached by the twenty-two-year-old son of the society lady who'd been lurking in the background with his friends. "Hey," he whispered. "Do you want to go to a club?"

And then it happened to Queenie. She hired a twenty-four-year-old intern for the summer. He'd barely worked past Fourth of July before he confessed that he found her incredibly sexy and tried to kiss her.

Which made me wonder: Are middle-aged women now catnip for younger men?

At first the idea seemed impossible. After all, for years, the very idea that a younger man would be attracted to a woman ten, twenty, even thirty years older was unimaginable—to the point where it was nearly considered a crime against nature.

Plus, while there are a zillion movies depicting the older man/much younger woman dynamic, for decades there was only one movie depicting the opposite: *The Graduate.*

However, unlike the older man/younger woman movie thing where they ride off into the sunset to live (somehow given their thirty-year age difference) happily ever after, *The Graduate* turns out to be pretty *bad* for everyone involved.

The message of this movie is clear: ladies, don't you ever, ever, ever try this at home.

And so, for about twenty years, no self-respecting woman did, until the eighties came along. Suddenly, there were "cougars"—older women who dared to have sex or at least be attracted to hot young men who were called boy toys—often depicted as pumped-up young men in black shorty shorts and greased muscles. Everyone made fun of them and rightly so: they were ridiculous. You'd look at them and wonder: If I have sex with a boy toy how will I get that greasy-thick Vaseline mixed with sweat off my sheets in the morning?

Now another thirty years have passed. And thanks to pornography, things have changed. In 2007, the most googled porn request was "MILF"—mothers I'd like to fuck.

In other words, there is now a whole generation of young men who've been turned on by the idea, at least, of sex with a woman twenty and possibly thirty years older.

And why not? Due to exercise, hair extensions, Botox and filler, healthy eating, and advanced skin care, even if a woman is technically too old to bear a child, she can still look like she can.

Making her the perfect candidate for a cubbing experience.

Catnips versus Cougars

Instead of being about older women in pursuit of younger men—like it was in *The Graduate*—cubbing is about younger men in pursuit of older women. And while the word "cougar" conjures the stereotype of a hardened woman who dresses too young for her age, catnips tend to be nice, practical women from the city, the suburbs, anywhere really, and they are very, very likely to be someone's *mom from school.*

But then something happens, and all of a sudden a sensible woman finds herself in the middle of an unintended cub situation.

Take Joanne. She was attending a dinner at Queenie's house when it happened. Queenie had hired a chef. Like so many situations these days in which millennials are doing the jobs much older people used to do, the chef was twenty-seven. Joanne and the chef happened to look into each other's eyes, and *bam.*

Unintended cub collision.

Perhaps it all would have been fine—if the guy hadn't been Queenie's niece's boyfriend. Queenie was understandably pissed. Joanne said he was fair game. Sides were taken. But who knows what the etiquette is even supposed to *be* in this situation?

I ran into Joanne in the city three months after she'd been caught with the cub. I assumed she and the cub had parted ways.

Nope. The opposite was true.

She was not only dating him, but he had also been living in her apartment for the past three months. "We were shacking up," she said with a little shrug. "It was really, really fun." But now, she informed me, he was getting his own place.

She looked a little embarrassed and vulnerable. I could see that she'd let herself fall in love with him and no doubt was wondering if the fact that he was getting his own place meant he was about to break up with her. I could feel her shame: at fiftysomething, shouldn't we all know better by now?

Absolutely not. A few more months passed and Kitty ran into them shopping for appliances. They were still together.

Because in the new world of cubbing, some men do stick around. Or even worse, fall in love.

And yet, not all cubbing goes so smoothly. From your first unexpected cub pounce to housing your cub in the Cub Club and then to the possibility of walking down the aisle—look at you with your younger husband—there are lots of horrifying pitfalls along the way. Like: what if you wake up with a cub at "his" house and it turns out you know his parents?

Oops. This nearly happened to Tilda Tia a month ago.

You don't want it to happen to you.

La Cubbette—C'est Vous

What's tricky about this cubbing phenomenon is that it can happen to any woman, even a woman who has never considered the idea of being with a younger man.

Take Kitty. All her life, she's been attracted to older men. Ten, fifteen, even twenty years older, like her soon-to-be ex-husband. "I like men who are intelligent. Who have something to say. I can't imagine finding that in a twenty-five-year-old."

Little did we know how quickly she'd change her mind.

It happened at a small birthday party for one of Kitty's still-married friends. This married friend, Alison, was someone Kitty had spent a lot of time with when she was married. She was also one of the few friends from Kitty's former married life who still invited her to parties.

After six months, Kitty was beginning to realize that all those nasty things people told you about being divorced were true: friends took sides and you kept hearing about gatherings you were no longer invited to.

At the party, Kitty tried to reassure these still-married couples that she was okay and doing fine. They tried to reassure her, too. The men took her aside and told her that they'd always thought her ex-husband was a jerk, while the women crowded around her in the kitchen and told her she would find someone better.

During dinner, the talk once again turned to Kitty and her new relationship status. There was lots of clueless married talk about online dating and whether or not it worked and whether or not Kitty should try it.

Kitty found herself getting more and more depressed. She was trying to figure out if there was any way she could leave the dinner before the birthday cake was served. She could claim a sudden stomach bug or other vague illness, maybe even cry that something had happened to her dog—when suddenly the door opened and a posse of young twentysomething guys came through the door.

This sudden injection of male hormones was like heroin hitting the mainframe. The atmosphere immediately changed. It became lively. The middle-aged folks sat up a little straighter, their conversation became more pointed and jovial and even louder.

It was as if the adults were suddenly vying for the attention of the young men.

Kitty quickly surmised that the shorter cute one was Alison's now twenty-three-year-old son, Mason, whom she hadn't seen since he was about twelve. The other guys were Mason's friends. Not wanting to interrupt the parents, they bade their goodbyes and said they were going to hang out downstairs in the finished basement.

The adults moved into the living room. The talk turned to vacations, a meaningless pursuit that Kitty could no longer afford. She kept glancing toward the open door, wondering how to make her escape. It was during one of these glances that she spotted Mason and two of his buddies slithering by on their way into the kitchen.

Kitty cleared her throat and laughed politely. She put down her espresso in its ungainly cup and stood up. She'd made it halfway to the door when the host noticed. He must have once been handsome or hottish. But he wasn't now.

"Kitty," he demanded, with an inappropriate note of male authority she hadn't heard from him before, as if now that she were single, he somehow had dominion over her. "Where are you going?" he asked.

"Bathroom," Kitty said.

She headed toward it but kept right on going when she realized she could get to the kitchen with no one in the living room being the wiser.

She went for it.

"Hey," Mason said.

"Sorry," Kitty said. "I was just looking for some water."

The hottest one—the tall one with the swooping dark hair—smiled at her politely and, looking her right in the eye, said, "I'll help you."

He opened the refrigerator, removed a Fiji water, and handed it to her.

Kitty paused. "What I'd really like is a shot of tequila," she said.

There was dead silence, and then the guys laughed like they genuinely thought she was funny.

Mason said, "You're the only fun one of my mom's friends."

And suddenly, Kitty began to feel better.

Why else would she agree to go downstairs?

The Unexpected Cub Pounce

And downstairs is where she went, down to the old rec room, which was exactly what she used to do back when she was a teenager.

These kids, of course, weren't teens. They were young adults. And the wreck room wasn't some beat-up couch with an old Ping-Pong table. It was three thousand square feet with a Ping-Pong table, screening room, and wet bar. There was music and beer. Two other girls had arrived. Kitty knew their mothers. One of them got Kitty a beer.

Kitty took the beer and went over to talk to Mason and his friend. They were smoking something and Kitty asked what it was and it was a vaporizer. When they offered it to her, she thought about how she had to get upstairs and she pictured the scene: the safe middle-aged faces she'd known forever. She took the vape.

Mason's friend kept talking to her. He touched her forearm a couple of times, but she was sure it must be a mistake and she had mistaken it. She reminded herself that she had to get back upstairs. "I've got to go," she said vaguely, looking around for Mason. "I've got to say goodbye."

And she would have, if Mason's friend hadn't talked her into a game of Ping-Pong and another puff on the vape.

And then, somehow, somewhere along the vast walk from Ping-Pong table to staircase, the guy tried to kiss her.

In fact, he did kiss her. His hands were suddenly on her face and his lips felt fat and young and he was actually making out with her and she was making out with him back!

But then she remembered where she was and what she was doing. If someone found out, there would be no explaining it to Alison. And there would be repercussions.

She pushed the guy away. He looked disappointed but let her go. She went quickly upstairs and into the bathroom, where she smoothed her hair and checked her watch. A half hour had passed! Surely someone would have noted her absence.

But as she slunk back into the living room, she soon discovered that no one had noticed at all. They were too intent on discussing the latest political transgression in Washington.

Meanwhile, Kitty kept going over the cub pounce in her head. The kiss had made her second-guess her desire for only older men.

What was happening to her?

Kitty got up to go, and when she did, the young people magically appeared from downstairs. It turned out they had to go, too.

Indeed, it turned out that what they really needed Kitty for was a ride. To a nightclub.

Like so many millennials, these kids had forgotten something. In this case, getting their driver's license.

And here's the problem with inexperienced cubbing: can you imagine what would have happened if Kitty had continued to make out with the cub and then it turned out he was only using her as someone to drive him around?

Alison would have been furious. And Kitty's social life as she knew it would have definitely gone kaput.

We can all learn a few things from Kitty's experience.

A woman is vulnerable to a UCP (unexpected cub pounce) if she: (a) is recently divorced or separated from her partner, (b) hasn't had much male attention in the last few years, or

(c) does something she normally doesn't do or hasn't done for a long time, i.e. vaping.

But unlike Kitty's near-miss, not every cub pounce is unsuccessful. Indeed, for the uninitiated, a cub pounce can often lead to a full cub encounter, involving intercourse, or at least its possibility. And once again, in this new dating arena there are lessons to be learned. Just because a cub is young and willing, it doesn't mean it's a good idea.

Beware the Cub Romeo

Witness what happened to Tilda Tia when she went to a party at a club in Southampton. There were a whole bunch of young people at this party and she met one of them and he was tall, fairly attractive, and possibly rich. When the cub pounced, she went with it. It should have been over quickly, but the cub turned out to be excessively emotional, in that way that only twentysomethings can be. He insisted that he was madly in love with her and began texting her fifteen times a day to see what she was up to and whom she was with. Then he tried to leave a suitcase full of clothes in her bedroom. Then he invited her to meet his parents.

Specifically at Sunday lunch. At an address Tilda Tia knew well having gone there many times for lunch before— *twenty-five years ago when she'd been friends with his parents before the cub was born.*

No. This was not going to happen. She was not going to date the son of her friends even if she hadn't seen them for a while. She texted the cub: *I'm breaking up with you right now.*

Unfortunately, the cub was a Romeo type, so this go-away technique only made him fall in love further and he went over to Tilda Tia's and demanded that she give him another chance. They had a big confrontation and finally the only way she could get rid of him was by locking the door and throwing his cell phone out her second-story window.

Meaning the cub nearly turned Tilda Tia into something she'd never been before: a character more crazy than anyone from *The Real Housewives.*

Never Ever Go Back to a Cub's House at Night—You Don't Know What You'll Find.

This happened to Marilyn. She'd gotten used to her Netflix nights at home on Saturday evenings, absorbed in what appeared to be more interesting narratives than her own. But as occasionally happens, some friends from Miami came to visit her in the Village and naturally they wanted to go out. Which meant that Marilyn was going to have to go out, too.

This was a bummer. Marilyn, used to having all her time to herself, hadn't bathed for three days. Hadn't washed her hair for a week. Hadn't bought new clothes for at least a year.

But she had to make the effort.

The friends from Miami wanted to hit all the famous Village hot spots. At first Marilyn felt bored and out of place and kind of self-conscious. But then her friends were doing shots of tequila and she did, too. They started playing darts. Marilyn went back to the bar for another round and struck up a conversation with the bartender. Mike was no older than twenty-five, but it turned out that he and Marilyn were actually from the same city in Australia. Then he asked her if she wanted to go out back.

No one else was paying attention to her so Marilyn figured: Why not?

The Australian then proceeded to kiss her next to the Dumpsters.

Back inside, he gave her a free shot of tequila. Then he asked if she wanted to go to his house to smoke weed.

At this point, Marilyn was drunk enough to agree that this sounded like a good idea.

The cub's "house" turned out to be a seriously dilapidated Airstream trailer.

Marilyn did her best to admire the patched linoleum floor, the depressing late-1970s design. There was a table set between built-in plastic benches covered with young-man detritus: a bong, a speaker, a cactus, various small tins, dirty coffee cups. Mike sat down and started rolling a spliff, pasting two papers together and expertly twirling them into a cone into which he shoveled a mixture of tobacco and weed.

"What do you think of my crib?" he asked. "Cool, huh?"

"Yes, very cool," Marilyn said, wondering if she hung out with him if she'd have to start saying words like "crib," too. "Where do you sleep?"

"Over there," Mike said, indicating a stained mattress leaning against the wall. As he licked the paper and made a nice twist at the tip, Marilyn realized she couldn't do this. She could not have sex with a guy on a bare mattress in a dilapidated Airstream trailer from the 1970s.

She had to draw the line.

Mike, however, wasn't happy about this. "Why?" he asked. "Is it because you don't like me?"

"I think you're a really terrific guy. But"—she paused and then played the cub trump card—"I'm old enough to be your mother."

"You're older than my mother," Mike said.

And with that, Marilyn walked back to town, thanking her lucky stars for getting out of there before she really had something to feel bad about.

A Cautionary Tale: Always Check a Cub's Credentials

If you're going to cub, you want to be smart about it. Because you're older and wiser, you know that sometimes cubs do really dumb things.

And sometimes, you can be the victim of a dumb cub. Or even worse: a cub con.

This is what happened to Mia.

Mia's husband, Brian, was a multimillionaire hedge fund guy and Mia was his third wife. On her fiftieth birthday, Brian threw Mia a huge party under a tent with pink lights and a dance floor and a performance by a pop star. Then he gifted her with a diamond necklace and said he wouldn't be the man he was today without her.

A month later, he went to Vegas, met a twenty-one-year-old dancer and fell "in love." Two months later, he set his dancer up in an apartment on the Upper East Side not far from where he and Mia lived. Four months later, his new love was pregnant.

Mia and Brian had an airtight prenup: In case of divorce, Mia would get a lump sum of thirty million dollars. She would also get the house in the Hamptons and could keep all her jewelry, which was estimated to be worth at least five million dollars on its own.

And because Brian was well-known in the financial world and had behaved in a manner that was, according to those who knew him, completely out of character, the divorce ended up in the gossip columns. Along with the particulars of the settlement.

Mia escaped to the house in the Hamptons. Two sisters and a handful of friends rushed to her side. They came and went for the next few weeks, but then there was a lull and Mia was on her own.

But not quite. Because Mia's house had all the fixings—heated swimming pool, extensive gardens, and a tennis court—there were always people around.

✳   ✳   ✳

One afternoon when Mia was lying out by the pool, her sister called. As usual, the conversation centered on Brian and what a terrible man he'd turned out to be and how Mia should have somehow known this would happen. Meanwhile, two guys arrived on the property to check the air-conditioning units.

When Mia hung up she noticed that one of them was standing just a few feet away. He was an unusually handsome kid with bright eyes and enticing lips. It briefly crossed Mia's mind that he was too young and too cute to have already settled on a career fixing air conditioners.

"We're finished," he said.

"Terrific." Mia gave him a polite smile.

But instead of turning away, he hesitated as if he wanted to ask her something.

"Yes?" Mia said.

He suddenly held out his hand. "I'm Jess, by the way."

"Mia," she said. She noticed that his palm felt soft and friendly.

He smiled in a manner that Mia thought indicated he knew he was good-looking and was confident that his looks were a ticket to something better. "I couldn't help overhearing a bit of your conversation. Are you married to—" He blurted out Brian's name with reverence.

Mia stiffened. Hearing Brian's name come out of this kid's mouth was like a slap. Her anger toward Brian and by extension anyone who knew him, including this kid, was freshly aroused along with her suspicions. Why on earth was this kid asking about Brian? Did he know him? Had Brian sent the kid here to spy on her?

"I was," she said coldly. "Why?"

"I just wanted to let you know that he's my idol."

At first, this didn't make sense. Brian was someone's idol? How could that be? But it could, easily, Mia thought. There was always some misguided kid ready to worship at the altar of money.

Mia suddenly lost it. "My husband is a shithead," she snapped.

She immediately regretted saying it, because the kid, Jess, began apologizing profusely for mentioning Brian's name.

This was its own kind of agony. Jess was young and insecure, and it took her at least ten minutes to reassure him that it was okay, she was okay, and no, she wasn't angry at him and he wasn't going to lose his job.

He finally left, exiting through a side gate located behind a strip of hedges where it was difficult to see who was coming or going.

Mia went into the kitchen, passing one of the two live-in housekeepers who was on her way to the store. They briefly discussed the air conditioners, which reminded Mia of the conversation she'd had with the guy about Brian. As she poured herself more wine, she noticed that her hand was shaking in anger.

"Mia?"

Mia nearly dropped the glass as she turned to find that Jess had not only returned but was standing in the kitchen.

"I'm sorry. I forgot something. Are you okay?" he asked.

"Do I look okay?" Mia said, glaring at him as she took a gulp of wine, hoping the alcohol would help her regain control. It didn't. Instead, when Jess took a step forward and asked what Brian did to her, Mia, who had been telling the story over and over again to her friends by rote, told him the whole terrible tale with all the intimate details.

It wasn't until the housekeeper returned that Jess finally left, saying he or someone else would be back in a few days to make sure the air-conditioning unit was working properly.

Mia spent those days drinking rosé and talking on the phone. Sometimes she went through a bottle by 6:00 p.m., at which time her head hurt and she could blessedly pass out for a few hours. And indeed, on the afternoon when Jess came back to check on the unit, Mia had gone through nearly a bottle.

She was a little pissed and a little pissed off. She followed him out to the side of the house where the massive units were hidden behind cypress trees. She asked him why Brian was his idol and Jess explained that Brian gave money to a scholarship fund at his school to encourage kids like him to go into business.

And now he had. He was also studying at Southampton College. And when he wasn't working or in school, he was surfing. He told Mia she should take up surfing and she laughed and said she would think about it. And once again, Mia found herself shaking. This time, not with anger but with a sudden and unexpectedly strong desire for Jess.

Two days later Mia was at the liquor store buying a case of rosé when she ran into Jess in the parking lot. He asked if she was having a party and she said no, a few friends were coming over and they liked to drink.

Out of an obligation to be nice she told herself, Mia invited him to stop by for a drink sometime.

And maybe out of an obligation to be nice back, he put her number in his phone.

The next evening, around 7:00 p.m., when Mia was lying in bed watching a reality show on Bravo, her phone buzzed.

A text: *Hey, it's Jess.*

Mia's mood immediately lifted. *Hi Jess,* she wrote back.

You around? Want to hang?

Sure, Mia wrote, not caring that she couldn't even be bothered to be coy.

Neither could Jess. They hadn't gone through a glass of wine before he put his hands on either side of Mia's face and began kissing her. Mia expected herself to resist but instead was shocked by how instantly she was aroused—a sensation she hadn't known she could still experience.

After a short make out session, Jess took her hand and guided her upstairs into an empty guestroom. He took off his clothes and so Mia took off hers as well. Then he went into the bathroom, turned on the shower, and beckoned for her to join him.

He leaned over—he was at least eight inches taller than she was, which was amazing considering Brian had been two inches shorter—and they began making out again while soaping each other's bodies. Another thing Mia hadn't done in a very long time. Then he bundled her up into a towel and spun her around and out of the towel, which he laid down on the bed.

He leaned over her again, kissing her until she was beneath him.

And then it was like being in a porn film. He performed cunnilingus, his tongue darting here and there, then turned her around for the sixty-nine. His cock was shortish and fat, but before she could really get to it, he lay back and reached for the condom he had at the ready. He rolled it on and pulled her forward to mount him. She rubbed the top of his penis against her vagina, feeling for the magic opening where he could slip in without jarring. He gave a jerk of his hips and in he went and Mia began rocking her pelvis, feeling him inside and feeling—for the first time in a long time—confident. As if she were kind of an expert. Like she really could be in a porn film.

Ride 'em, cowgirl, she thought.

And then he came when she was almost ready to come but didn't. But it was okay she reassured him. She would, next time.

He left ten minutes later. Mia was too wiped out to notice or actually care.

Two weeks passed and then three. Three weeks in which Mia didn't see or hear from Jess. At first, she was angry. But the emotion faded. She told herself she shouldn't have been surprised. Men sucked, and Jess was just another example.

She went back to the rosé bottle, which didn't disappoint, and dove deep.

A rare text pulled her out of her stupor.

Hey, it said. *Want to hang?*

Jess! She'd nearly forgotten about him. And once again, she couldn't believe how excited she was to hear from him. She texted back: *When?*

He replied immediately. *I'm with my bud. We'll come by in twenty.*

Jess's friend Drew was kind of creepy, but Mia did her best to ignore him in favor of this opportunity to see Jess. She got drunk quickly. They all did. Then Drew left and she and Jess went upstairs. "I'm not going to do this," Jess said. "You're too wasted."

This was the last thing Mia wanted to hear. "I'm not wasted. Come on," she said, shocked by the note of desperation in her voice.

Jess hesitated but not for long. He took off his pants and Mia put her hand around his penis, noting once again his super-hard hard-on that only the young possessed.

But this time the sex was over far too quickly, and before Mia could stop him, he was gone. She grabbed a bottle of wine and went back to bed. And once again, before long, it was six in the morning and her head hurt like hell. She gulped some water and took another half of a sleeping pill.

A week later, at two in the afternoon, Jess showed up at the house with Drew again.

Mia, who couldn't be bothered to pretend anymore, opened a fresh bottle of wine and poured them each a glass. They sat down at the kitchen table.

"So listen, Mia," Drew said. "We have a problem."

"We do?" This wasn't what Mia was expecting. She didn't think she knew either one of these guys well enough to have "a problem" with them.

"Jess told me what happened," Drew said.

"What are you talking about?" Mia looked at Jess questioningly.

"He's underage," Drew said.

"Excuse me?" Mia's first instinct was to hide the wine. If Jess was underage, he shouldn't be drinking. She looked guiltily at the glass in front of him. "Why didn't you tell me?"

"You didn't ask," Jess said.

So Mia did ask for proof. Drew claimed that Jess left his license at home. Mia asked Jess how he could do this to her and Jess looked scared and wouldn't speak.

Drew got to the bottom line. He and Jess were going to blackmail her and wanted at least a hundred thousand dollars.

They knew how rich she was. They'd read about her divorce settlement in the papers. And now she'd had sex with Jess, who was underage, and if she didn't pay she was going to be arrested.

For the next three days, Mia was in a panic. How could this happen to her? She longed to tell someone, but whom? Her girlfriends wouldn't understand. In fact, they'd be horrified. They'd say that this confirmed what they'd secretly suspected all along—that Mia was somehow a bad person who deserved to have terrible things happen to her.

But then it wouldn't matter, because she'd be arrested. Her photograph would go viral. Her life would be over.

A couple of days later, Jess's boss came by. He was a nice guy from a few towns over, married with a couple of grown kids who still lived in the Hamptons. He was a talker, and before long, probably because there was no one else she could tell, Mia told him what had happened with Jess.

He was furious. He knew Jess well. Jess had gone to high school with his daughter. Jess had been telling the truth when he said he was in college. He was twenty not seventeen.

A couple of days later, Jess came over to apologize. It wasn't his idea he said. It was Drew's. He'd been boasting to Drew about how cool it was that he was having sex with his idol's ex-wife and then Drew jokingly came up with this plan and Jess thought he was kidding but Drew was fucking crazy and he definitely wasn't talking to that kid ever again.

Mia forgave him. Partly because she was a nice person and partly because she just couldn't stand to listen to Jess and his lame excuses anymore.

Mia did eventually tell her friends, and they had a good laugh about it. In the end, Mia was like most middle-aged women whose cub adventure would become just another one of the bizarre and inexplicable things that would happen to them in the next few years.

Others, however, take their cubbing to the next stage.

The Cub Club

This happens when a woman moves from what she assumes will be a one or two time event to a more regular arrangement. The cub begins to spend the night. Now there is a very good chance he will move in.

And there he is, suddenly living in your house.

Some questions:

How do you introduce your cub to your friends? How do you explain why he's living with you after a month? What if your friends don't like him or, even worse, what if they just plain ignore him?

That's what happened to Sassy and me.

We were barely two weeks into June when James appeared.

He sat uncomfortably at the edge of the kitchen table at Kitty's, surrounded by the girls—Sassy, Tilda Tia, Marilyn, Queenie, me, and Queenie's teenage daughter.

I assumed he was a friend of Queenie's daughter. I didn't think about it much, because everyone was talking loudly, and as happens in these cases when one male is outnumbered by a bunch of women, James quietly disappeared into the background.

So imagine my surprise when I stopped by Sassy's place two days later and James was there.

It was noon and Sassy seemed a bit embarrassed, but she had a quick explanation. "James is helping me with my new phone."

I nodded. As I would later learn, becoming indispensably helpful—i.e., programing the iPhone, showing how to connect music, and even going for alcohol and food runs—is one of the sneaky moves cubs use in order to get a woman to house them.

But I wasn't thinking about it at the time. Indeed, I didn't think about it again until Sassy had a barbeque and James was there. Again. He'd brought the meat. But still.

James was starting to annoy me slightly. Was he always going to be there? And why? He was at least twenty, twenty-five years younger than we were. What the hell could be so interesting about a bunch of middle-aged women doing their own thing that would make him want to hang around?

The next day, Tilda Tia and I went for a bike ride. I immediately asked her about James. What did she know about him?

Tilda Tia shrugged. "He's a real estate agent."

"He's old enough to have a job?"

"He's almost thirty. He broke up with his girlfriend four months ago, so I guess he's bored."

I didn't ask how old the girlfriend was. Instead, I asked her how Sassy had met him. I could have asked Sassy myself, but something about the situation prevented me.

Tilda Tia was vague. She mentioned something about an evening at a club, back in the days when she was still cubbing. Tilda Tia was no longer cubbing herself and had instead moved on to Tinder.

Another month passed. Every time I saw Sassy at a party, I was surprised and annoyed that James was still hanging around. He would get her drinks and seemed to be on friendly terms with all of our friends. I was suspicious. But when I asked around, everyone said they "loved" James. He was handy and he was happy to be the designated driver.

And then it was casually mentioned that he was staying at Sassy's. For the moment, anyway. He'd had a share in another house, but it was only for one month. So now he and his VW bug were temporarily parked in Sassy's driveway.

This is another typical cub ploy: suddenly moving in when they've lost a place to live.

Like James, the cub always claims to have a place to live when you first meet. Then the "place to live" becomes someplace less defined—a place to "crash" perhaps. And then the place mysteriously disappears altogether and the cub is homeless.

And where better to stay than with you?

Naturally the cub reassures—and cautions—that the arrangement is only temporary. Cubs know that the women who house them are not looking for forever. Forever is too soon. It's too raw, it's too scary. Especially when you don't know where you'll be three months from now.

Which is why, perhaps, Sassy chose to keep it a secret.

Although I suspected that Sassy and James might be having conjugal relations, I couldn't really confirm it. There were no tipoffs, no tells. No sidelong glances. No handholding. No whispers in the hallway.

While Sassy and I were out talking on the deck, James would usually be in the house on internet central. I'd pass him on my way out and we'd wave hello. When Sassy and James did interact, a lot of it seemed to be about scheduling.

Was he some kind of assistant?

The day came when I skipped a bike ride with Tilda Tia and in the middle of the morning, having driven to town to post letters, I decided to pop over to Sassy's.

The cars were there, so I went inside. The place was empty. I wandered into Sassy's room just to be sure.

The bed was a mess, and the pillows on both sides had been used. On the floor was a torn packet of foil.

Was I the only one who didn't know?

"Why didn't you tell me?" I asked Tilda Tia later that day.

"Tell you what?" she said. As usual, she was distracted with Tinder and her next date.

"Sassy and James are not just friends. They're *sleeping together*." I said this thunderously, as if I were Charlton Heston in one of those religious movies.

"So?"

"She never told me they were."

"She didn't tell me either," Tilda Tia said. "Which means if she didn't tell us she doesn't want us to know."

"Fine. We know nothing," I said. Nevertheless, I was determined to ask Sassy myself.

"Are you and James . . ." I could barely bring myself to say the words.

"Do you think I'm going to end up with a guy who's twenty-five years younger than I am? Come on," Sassy said.

Sassy quietly unhoused her cub at the end of the summer.

And perhaps, in keeping with the clandestine nature of her cubbing adventure, Sassy and James are still friends. James is going to visit soon and he's bringing his new girlfriend. Sassy can't wait to meet her. And neither can we.

The Future

What we don't know about older women/younger men relationships is a lot. In fact, we hardly know anything at all, mostly because there haven't been enough of these relationships to draw any significant conclusions.

But it is likely there will be more and more of them in the future. At least according to the internet, which is filled with sites exploring the older woman/younger man dynamic. Sure, some of the couples look like models, but more often it's just regular women like Meegan, forty-two, who has her own vlog and sums up the reverse-age romance like this: "Hey ladies, you've tried the younger woman/older man thing, and how's that working out for you—*huh?*"

The future of cubbing is wide open.

CHAPTER FIVE

THE FIFTEEN-K FACE CREAM, THE RUSSIANS, AND ME

"WHERE'S YOUR apartment?" people would ask. "The Upper East Side," I'd reply, and they'd roll their eyes. The Upper East Side wasn't cool. It was boring and shut down after sundown and there were too many strollers and too many old people and so no one interesting lived there. On the other hand, the fact that no hipsters or groovy people wanted to be seen there made the apartment, by New York City standards, somewhat affordable.

Unfortunately, it was the only thing in my immediate neighborhood that was.

Welcome to Madison World

I discovered this on my second morning when I set out to take a stroll. I hadn't gone half a block when I passed a window display of glasses and, reminded that I could use a new pair, went inside.

With burled wood walls and cases decorated with cigar boxes, the small shop was more like a gentleman's club where they happened to sell spectacles. A dapper young man came over and asked if I wanted to see anything. I pointed to a pair of tortoiseshell frames. I replaced my glasses with the empty frames. But I then had no idea how I looked, because without my glasses I was blind, like Piggy in *Lord of the Flies*.

"I don't know," I said. "How much are they?"

"Three thousand dollars," he said casually, as if this were the going price for frames all over the world.

Three thousand dollars? Again?

"And then you have to add in the cost of the actual lenses. That's another thousand each."

In other words, five thousand dollars for glasses.

"Great," I said, backing away with a big smile on my face.

I left the store feeling self-conscious. I didn't belong in this neighborhood and everyone in the neighborhood knew it.

Madison World, I called it. Located between Fifth and Park, it was an Aladdin's cave of gold and silver, of diamonds and jewel-encrusted watches, of crocodile shoes and dresses scattered with hand-embroidered crystals. In Madison World, women dressed in outrageous fashions and paraded up and down the street like it was the most glamorous runway in the world.

They knew I was an interloper. They could tell by my creased cotton pants, both practical and comfortable. They knew by my hair, untouched for weeks by the smoothing heat of the blow-dryer. But mostly they knew by my shoes—Havaianas flip-flops.

I was going to have to learn how to dress again.

Madison World Sticker Shock

You'd think I'd do the obvious thing: go into a store on Madison Avenue and just buy something. But shopping in Madison World doesn't work that way. It's a complicated process. There's a lot of interaction with other humans who are there to decide whether or not they are going to sell you their wares, whether or not you can afford them, and whether or not you should even be seen in them. Purchasing something in Madison World is like trying to get your kid into an exclusive private school.

Actually, the private school process might be more pleasant because you don't have to get undressed in front of strangers.

But first you have to find something to try on.

This is not as easy as it sounds. Expensive clothes are often chained to their racks like packhorses at a dude ranch. This is not to discourage stealing, which would be all too apparent given the fact that these "clothes" are often elaborate affairs that can't easily be hidden, in, say, a regular shopping bag. No. The clothes are chained as a stern reminder that you're not really supposed to handle them. You will need the assistance of a wrangler before you can even get close to getting them into the dressing room.

If you're not already a tich intimidated, you might be when you see the dressing room itself. Chances are it's more expensively furnished than your apartment. It may have a couch or two and definitely a few throw pillows. You can see how someone really rich might be encouraged to have an afternoon party there.

And this brings us to the best part of shopping in Madison World: You can drink. Most stores serve champagne. And unlike the exorbitant prices that restaurants charge, the champagne in Madison World is free.

You'll want some of that champagne for Dutch courage. In addition to the couches, the dressing room likely has a platform centered in front of a large, three-sided mirror. You may be able to survive your own gaze, but can you survive the gaze of the entire sales staff? Because while you are changing, you will inevitably get that knock on the door. "How are you doing?"

What the wrangler really means is: How are the clothes doing?

The ordeal is far from over, however. If you do "find something" you want to take home, you will have to purchase it. Everywhere else in the world this is done with a touch of a button. Not in Madison World.

For some strange reason, it will take at least fifteen minutes to ring up your purchase and run your credit card. During this time, exhausted, you may collapse on one of the many divans—or fainting couches—located near the opening in the wall where the salespeople disappear to make this mysterious, time-consuming transaction.

And then you have to pay the bill. It's always more than you feared. Walking into a store in Madison World is like walking into a casino. You have no idea how much money you might lose.

But behind the glittering cases of jewels and fine leathers and backgammon sets with mother-of-pearl inlay was an ugly secret: the stores in Madison World were going broke.

It was a refrain I'd overhear again and again, made by everyone from the salespeople taking a break out on the street to the bartender at Bar Italia.

Still, maybe the news wasn't all bad. If the stores were going broke, then certainly the stores should be having sales. Wasn't that the first rule of business? If something isn't selling, *maybe it's too expensive.*

I decided to make my first stop Ralph Lauren. There was usually some kind of good sale at Ralph. A year ago, I'd bought the one nice thing I now owned—a leather biker jacket—at 80 percent off. I wore it everywhere, and I happened to be wearing it when I walked in.

It may have been a twenty-four-hour news cycle of disaster out in the real world, but entering the store was like stepping into another time when nothing particularly bad was happening. The air smelled slightly of candy. Some kind of groovy music was playing—a boppy tune familiar enough to make me feel younger and like I had my whole future ahead of me. It was rather like being inside an egg.

The feeling didn't last long.

I was immediately surrounded by a flotilla of salespeople who recognized the leather jacket.

"I remember that jacket from last season. I always loved it."

"Have you seen this season's version?"

"Um, no. But how many does one woman need?" I said, as politesse forced me to examine the studded leather jacket that had been procured from the racks and was now being held out like a newly born child. I caught a glimpse of the price tag. Five thousand dollars. No wonder they were after me. How were they to know that there was no way I could afford a five-thousand-dollar jacket and that the one I had on had been 80 percent off?

I looked toward the entrance, hoping to make an escape, but the salespeople were blocking my way. What everyone said about the stores going broke must be true. Which meant the salespeople must be desperate.

The question was how desperate? And what would they do to me when they discovered I was a "fake" shopper? I imagined a scene like something out of *Invasion of the Body Snatchers.*

I tried to slip upstairs, but two salespeople followed me.

"Is there something you'd like to see?"

My eye was immediately drawn to the shiniest, most glittery piece in the room—an enormous ball gown constructed of tulle. I hurried toward it, hoping I might hide behind the vast skirts.

No dice.

"Can I help you?" the saleswoman asked.

"Just wondering about the price," I murmured.

"What would you like to know?"

"How much is it?"

The salesperson went to the dress and turned over the tag.

I held my breath while I did a few quick calculations. Twenty years ago, that dress would have been thirty-five hundred dollars. Allowing for "inflation" it would be about five thousand today. But then there's the rich tax.

"Rich tax" is the price you pay for being rich in the first place. If there's one thing that most people don't understand about the rich it's that there's nothing they like more than fleecing other rich people. It's why the richer the rich get, the more expensive everything they need to buy to prove they're part of the richy-rich club—the yachts, the Hamptons homes, the clothes—goes up in price as well.

And so, given the rich tax, I guessed the dress would be eight thousand dollars.

Wrong. "Twenty thousand dollars," said the saleswoman.

I gasped. That made the rich tax about twelve thousand dollars. It also made the dress out of reach for all but the richest of the rich. The point zero, zero I percent.

"Twenty thousand dollars," I exhaled. "That's the price of a small car. Who on earth can afford that?"

The salesperson looked around to make sure we weren't being overheard. "You'd be surprised who can afford it."

"Who?"

"I can't say," she whispered. "Hey, do you want to try it on?"

I shook my head.

"No. Because I'd never be able to afford it. Plus, I don't have anything to wear it to."

"You never know," the salesperson said.

And there it was. The mantra of the eternally hopeful. Buy this dress, take it home. Maybe this time the charm will work. Maybe this time it really will transform your life.

How Much Is That Doggie in the Window?

For weeks, I'd been limping along in an old pair of patent leather pumps that, while painful, weren't quite as painful as any of my other old shoes. I could last about two hours before I felt like my eyes were rolling into the back of my head from the agony.

"I can't," I finally said. "I can't walk."

It was time to buy a new pair of shoes. And since I didn't have a lot of money to throw around, I'd have to view the shoes as an investment.

Which meant the shoe would have to be a *staple*. A shoe that could go from day to night. From pants to a cocktail dress. It would be a shoe that fit. A shoe that I could *walk in*.

I thought I knew the very shoes.

They were black suede platforms with hand-stitched lacing. There was a rosette on top. Despite the rosette, there was something very solid, almost militaresque about the shoes.

This being Madison World, however, I couldn't just walk in, try them on, and buy them. As per the Ralph Lauren incident there was a protocol involved. Shoe salespeople are much nicer if you're already wearing an expensive pair of shoes, the idea being that if you already own a pair of expensive shoes, you can probably afford many, many others. And so I dug out a pair of flat-heeled designer booties I'd purchased just before I left the city. The boots weren't really my type of shoe, but I remembered that I was feeling confused about my life when I bought them. I'd just gotten divorced and wasn't sure how to proceed. The salesperson, a young man with pretty curling hair and excited puppy dog eyes, mentioned that Nicole Kidman had worn the same boots in an ad. He pointed to a poster on the wall as proof.

In the photograph, Nicole Kidman looked like a woman who knew where she was going and what she was doing. She was not a woman who was sad. She was not a woman who was alone, depressed, and felt like a failure. She was in control of her mind and her destiny.

I bought the shoes and tried to walk in them. But the proportions were all wrong. The boots made my legs look shorter and my feet bigger. They were long, narrow, nasty things that pinched terribly. I wore them twice and retired them.

Until now.

Sure enough, those suckers still hurt.

I winced into the store with a rictus grin. The shoe section was all the way in the back. A fifty-foot walk past the clothes I couldn't afford, past the fortysomething newly rich couple from Silicon Valley who could, and past the saleswomen who were trying to decide whether to help me or not. I said, "Erm, I'd like to see those shoes in the window?"

As usual, the salesperson asked which shoes, as if by forcing me back to the window and therefore the entrance, I might wander out of the store on my own—which I sometimes did.

But the shoes weren't there.

In fact, those shoes were so popular, another woman was trying on the only pair of eight and a halves left.

That was my size.

I don't know what kind of expression I had on my face, but the salesperson immediately took pity on me.

"They run small," she said. She was sure she had a size nine. They'd probably fit perfectly.

The woman who was trying on the eight and a halves was a classic Madison World lady. She appeared to be in her early forties but could have been older.

Her hair was Madison World blonde, a color not too platinum or too gold, in a tone that is cheerful without being showy. The texture is bouncy, of a length that can't be described as long or short. In other words, Madison World blonde is a pleasantly interchangeable hairstyle that looks good on many women and often causes them to look exactly alike, to the point where these women are often mistaken for other Madison World blondes, even by their own husbands.

No matter. Madison World blonde is an aspirational, achievable, and sisterly color. It allows women who have never met to instantly bond and become friends, secure in the knowledge that they probably have some other Madison World lady in common.

If I was going to fit in in Madison World, it was going to have to be some version of this. Which meant if the blonde was getting the shoes, I needed to have them as well.

The salesperson came back out. She only had a nine and a half left.

They would definitely be too large she said.

"I'm going to try them anyway," I said, countering with the universal line of female persuasion: "You never know."

She handed them over doubtfully.

I unwrapped the shoes and placed them on the carpet. I slipped my feet in. I rose up from my seat. Up and up and up. The shoes, which had somehow looked much lighter and more delicate in the window, were actually huge clomping affairs that would require Pilates-style leg muscles to maneuver across the landscape of uneven pavement, steps, grating, and other obstacles that had to be negotiated when walking in heels.

I took a step forward. Then another one. The shoes looked great and, at that moment, everyone in the store knew it.

"But they're too big," the saleslady said.

This was a little bit true. There was an eighth of an inch gap between my heel and the back of the shoe.

"I can call our other stores. See if anyone has a size nine."

"No," I said. "They're fine. *I can walk in them.*"

The triumph of having secured the right shoe triggered something in my brain, and then I couldn't stop shopping. When the fancy overpriced drugstore on the corner was going out of business with everything 50 percent off, I went on a mini spending spree. All of a sudden, I needed a whole bunch of things I hadn't thought about for ages. Like leather gloves. Makeup brushes. Six bottles of normally forty-dollar shampoo.

The penultimate splurge was a pair of hot-pink neoprene booties. I convinced myself it was okay to buy the booties because they were made of the same material as those swimming shoes, which also meant they were comfortable and a lot cheaper than leather.

They weren't entirely practical though. The color screamed: "Look at me." Out in the real world, when your clothes scream "look at me" you're supposed to be a six-foot model or at least an attractive young person. But I didn't live in the real world. I lived in Madison World, home to a variety of fashionistas. In addition to the Madison World lady and actual models was another type: an older woman in garb that would be considered bizarre and inappropriate anywhere else.

Up and down the avenue were women in neon colors and shiny gold accents. They wore head-to-toe black leather, lime-green tracksuits paired with platform sneakers, sequins and satin-striped pants that reminded me of the circus. And the hair. Dyed blonde mixed with sharp hues of bright pink and green and blue like peacock plumage. In true Madison World style, these birds of a feather stuck together. I'd see them congregating by a lamppost, smoking cigarettes. Or sitting outside Ladurée, in the green-and-white striped chairs eating pastel-colored macarons.

I was pretty sure these women weren't from Madison World, however. Proper Madison World ladies didn't laugh loudly with their girlfriends on the corner or scream into their cell phones. They didn't express excessive emotion in public. And mostly, they didn't smoke cigarettes, *much less smoke on the street.*

One day my curiosity got the better of me. When I saw a cluster of them standing in front of a store, I bummed a cigarette and stood close enough to overhear what they were saying.

They were Russians. Or Russian-speaking people. This was interesting. A well-placed source in Madison World had told me that the Russians were mostly responsible for the huge spike in the rich tax. They could afford to pay full price on dresses in the shops, which had driven up the cost.

Meanwhile, the Park Avenue princesses who were married to American billionaires were up in arms. Even they thought twenty thousand dollars was too much to pay for a party dress.

And now the Russians were all over Madison World. And they weren't just buying clothes.

The Russians Get Me

Meanwhile, with no other identity to choose from, I'd become that tired old urban cliché: the schlepper.

It had been years since I'd been a schlepper, but I remembered it well and not fondly. You carried it all with you—your work, your shoes, your life—in handbags the size of burlap sacks and worn department-store shopping bags and plastic grocery sacks. You became slightly stooped from the weight as you sherpa'd your way around dirty slush, toxic-looking deposits, strollers, bike messengers, up and down escalators and subway stairs worn dangerously smooth. You lugged your stuff from work to bars to clubs and to the bathroom in those clubs and eventually back to your tiny bedsit. Your back ached and your feet hurt, but you just kept on schlepping, hoping for the day when something magical would happen and you wouldn't have to schlep no more.

My schlepping route often took me straight through Madison World, past what appeared to be a group of Russian youths who hung out on the stoop in front of a store. They were attractive and had that careless air of kids who know they're cooler than you are. Sometimes they played music, but mostly they laughed and harassed passersby. I'd once seen them chase an unsuspecting woman to the corner, telling her they could help with her "sad eyes."

Every now and again a sinewy older guy who appeared to be in charge would come out and yell at them and tell them to get back to their real job: handing out free samples of face cream.

No thanks.

I hate taking samples. Hate having to make conversation with strangers. I managed to avoid the clutches of the Russians until one day one of the girls called out: "Hey, I like your style."

That stopped me in my tracks.

After all, who knew style better than these kids? All day long they stood outside, watching the fashionable people walk up and down the giant runway of Madison World.

Eventually, I struck up a passing acquaintance with these Russians. If I was in a good mood, I'd pass by and take a packet of face cream and talk about my dogs. If I was in a bad mood, I'd cross to the other side. While I'd see them ask other women to come inside the shop, I noted that they never asked me. I got the distinct sense they didn't think I was quite good enough for their face cream.

A day came when I was feeling particularly blue—too blue to cross to the other side. That middle-aged drumbeat of terror—it's all downhill from here!—was pulsing in my head. I was convinced that nothing good would ever happen again, that age was about to take away all of life's excitements and pleasures, leaving me with nothing but my own useless existence.

On that day, the day when they got me, I was also particularly laden with bags.

"You're so busy," called out the girl who'd said I had good style. We usually exchanged a few bon mots as I passed; she was the friendliest and not actually Russian but Greek.

I paused. For some reason, I wanted to explain. Yes, I was busy, but not doing anything particularly important.

"You've got to relax," said another.

They were right. I did need to relax. "You smoke?" asked the slim guy who was the most disdainful, perhaps because he looked like a male model. He held out a pack of foreign cigarettes.

They'd never offered me a cigarette before. I thought it would be rude to refuse, so I took it, while it crossed my mind that maybe they wanted to be friends with me.

"Hey!" said the Greek girl. "You're working so hard I'll give you a special treat."

"Really?"

"You want to get rid of the bags under your eyes?"

Hell yes.

She glanced over at the modelly guy, as if she needed his approval to "let me in." As though he were the de facto bouncer at this secret face cream club.

He looked me up and down, raised his eyebrows as if I were probably a lost cause, and nodded.

I was in!

The interior didn't disappoint. It was white and shiny, like one of those sleek stage sets on Broadway. Marble steps accented with gold led up to what could have been an actual small stage but instead contained the cash register.

I knew I'd made a mistake. This place was expensive—far too expensive for my budget. "I'm sorry. I can't."

"Come on. It will only take five minutes."

I balked. "Five minutes" in Madison World was fifteen or twenty anyplace else.

"You don't have five minutes?" she asked, as if this couldn't possibly be true. "Five minutes to look good for your boyfriend?"

I laughed. "I don't have a boyfriend."

"Maybe after you have this treatment you will."

She hustled me into a chair in front of the window. Having removed my glasses, she was now patting my face like I was a bunny. "Pretty," she said. "Why are you so pretty?"

This was an unanswerable question and one I immediately suspected she asked of all the women who took a seat in this chair. She pulled a giant syringe out of a drawer and, expurging a thick beige cream, patted it around the upper and lower lids of my left eye.

The result was like one of those magic science tricks—tiny dinosaurs that grow 1,000 percent in water—but the opposite.

Gone were the puffs and the lines. The skin around my eyes was miraculously smooth.

My mood immediately lifted. If I could get rid of my puffs that easily, perhaps I could get rid of all of my lines. Younger face, fresh life. Maybe it wasn't over after all. Maybe I could get on that big ride one more time.

The voice of Russian youth broke into my reverie: "Did you know we're having a special? Four hundred dollars for the product and then you get a free facial," said the modelly guy, who had strolled over to see the results.

"A facial, huh? You mean the whole face?"

I examined the skin around my eyes. If they had something that worked this well for the rest of my face, I was desperate to try it.

And so I bought the miracle depuffer cream for four hundred dollars and booked an appointment for the facial the next day at three. "You're lucky," said the older guy. "Krystal is here tomorrow. She will do your treatment."

"Who's Krystal?" I asked.

"She is the miracle worker of the skin."

"She's a goddess," agreed the modelly guy.

"She is the Mother Teresa of youth."

And on and on they went about this mysterious Russian woman named Krystal.

"All I can say is, whatever she tell you to do, you'd better do it!" exclaimed the older guy.

Fuck. What the hell had I gotten myself into?

Whatever it was, I woke up the next morning determined to get out of it. Apparently the Russians sensed I might do this, because at nine o'clock sharp, I got a call from the girl at the store.

She was confirming my appointment. She told me how lucky I was. Krystal was going to see me, and Krystal was going to change my life.

I didn't have the nerve to cancel.

I expected the treatment was going to be something high tech and slightly medical. Instead, I was led over to yet another lighted makeup counter where I took a seat on a revolving stool. I must have looked skeptical because the crew kept coming by to extoll Krystal's virtues. She was a skin genius. The older man informed me that I was very, very lucky that she happened to be in New York because she was almost never in New York.

"Where is she?"

"Traveling all over the world. She goes to California. Switzerland. Paris."

"And Russia? Right?" I said.

He gave me a funny look.

When they finally left me alone, I took off my glasses so I could see my phone. Krystal immediately came strolling out of a short open hallway.

She was very, very attractive. She was wearing a crisp white shirt, a black pencil skirt, and black pumps. She had white-blonde hair and eyes with light-blue irises encircled by a darker blue band. The tops of her breasts were visible through the open-necked collar of her shirt. She was carrying an iPad and a notebook, the kind you buy at the drugstore. There was a sharp air about her. She exuded purposefulness, as if she were playing a role.

She also had a pimple on her chin. I saw it when she leaned in to take a closer look at my skin.

The pimple worried me. Did she not use her own products? Did any of these kids use the products? Like me, they probably couldn't afford them. None of their skin was that great.

And neither was mine.

Krystal stepped back and looked at me sternly. "What kind of person are you?" she asked.

"Excuse me?"

"Are you the kind of person who can handle the truth?"

"I think so."

"I bet all your friends say you look good. This is true, yes?"

"They're my friends, so . . ."

"But I am not your friend. Not yet." Krystal sighed. "I'm going to be honest with you. Your skin looks bad."

For a moment, I was stung. Damn friends. Krystal was right. I sighed. "That's why I'm here. I need to look better."

Krystal tapped my face. "You have a little too much filler in the cheeks."

Every dermatologist said this and then went on to inject just a little more.

"And rosacea!"

Yes, I had that as well. So far nothing new here.

But there was good news. "If you do everything I tell you I can fix your face. Your skin will be perfect. I can make it go back in age twenty years."

Twenty years? That sounded like a tall order and probably not scientifically feasible. But I wasn't ready to give up yet.

"And you will not need to use Botox or fillers again," she added.

That jolted me. Botox and fillers are the twin posts on which "looking younger" rests. If there really were some face cream out there that worked like Botox, even I would have heard of it by now.

And then I realized I had.

Queenie had told me about it. How there were these people who got Upper East Side women to buy a whole bunch of products for thousands of dollars and they told them that *they'd never need Botox or filler again.*

Who would be so stupid as to believe that, I'd asked.

I was about to find out.

"I think I can help you," Krystal said. She bent over a bit the way younger people do when they think someone is older than they really are and maybe can't hear that well. My sight line was her cleavage. I quickly raised my eyes and stared into her eyes instead. "You have to promise me one thing."

"What?" I asked.

"If I tell you what to do, will you do it?"

I hesitated, wondering if I could politely make an escape, but at that moment, the Greek girl threw a cape around my shoulders and a towel was wrapped around my neck and covered with plastic. The stool was turned so that I faced the mirror.

Caped and toweled, separated from my glasses, I was a sitting duck. I widened my eyes and braced for what was to come.

What's Your Number?

"And now we will begin the treatment," Krystal said. She worked quickly, covering one-half of my face in a clay-like goop.

When she was finished, she stepped back so I could take a look. She put her head next to mine, like we were two girls in a Snapchat photo.

"We do one side of your face first and then the other. So you can see the results before and after. Exciting, yes?"

"Yes. Very exciting."

She sat down on her stool across from me. We smiled at each other.

"So," I said, after a moment. "How long for each side?"

She shrugged. "Twenty? Twenty-five minutes?" My heart sank. That meant I was stuck here for at least a full hour.

The thought was agony. I wasn't a big fan of beauty treatments because I didn't have the patience to sit through them. What the hell was I supposed to do for the next fifty minutes?

It didn't take long to find out.

Krystal picked up the pad of paper and a pencil and scooted closer. For a moment, I hoped she just wanted to make conversation. Instead she started asking me awkward questions about my finances.

How much money did I spend on Botox and filler a year?

"Two thousand dollars?" I asked.

She looked at me pityingly. "Most women spend twelve." She wrote something on the legal pad, which naturally I couldn't see.

"How much do you spend on your skin routine?"

"My routine?"

"Cleanser, toner. Facials. A thousand a month?"

Certainly not.

Krystal nodded and busied herself with the numbers. "Now this," she said, "is what you spend for one year for your face. And this"—she pointed to another number—"is what you spend over two years."

I didn't want to have to ask for my glasses and then put them on over the goop, so I did what I often do in these situations: I pretended I could see.

Besides, I could still read Krystal's body language. And clearly I was meant to exhibit surprise and outrage. I complied.

With a flourish, she put a slash through the numbers and started on a new page. "What would you say if I could make your skin better without Botox or filler and you never have to buy skin cream again for two years for half that price? And what if I said your skin could be twenty years younger in two years for even less than half of that? And what would you say if I could do all that for you and more. What would you pay for that?"

"I have no idea."

She wrote down a number and circled it like a pretend schoolteacher. I began to feel queasy. I was seriously out of my depth.

But how could that be? I was a grown woman in charge of my life and my pocketbook. Besides, how much could this damn face cream be?

She began grilling me about my habits. Did I have discipline? Did I know how to work a routine?

"A routine?"

"So you don't have one. If someone gives you a routine, would you do it?"

I probably absolutely would not. Maybe I was too lazy, but all I could think about was please don't give me another task. Please, don't give me another—probably pointless—thing to do.

"I guess I could try," I hedged.

"And what about instructions?"

"I can follow them."

"Because you have to do this facial once a month."

"What facial?" I was confused.

"I will teach you how to do it. And now we do the activation cream. It's going to be a little hot."

She rubbed a clear gel over the goop. It immediately began to heat up.

"Do you feel the heat?" she asked. "Do you feel it?"

"Yes?"

"It means the product is working."

"So this really works?"

She gave me a look. "Of course it works."

She produced "evidence." Before and after photos on her iPad that she accessed through a link.

"We are not supposed to show them but"—she glanced around furtively—"I will show them to you."

I wondered if this was some kind of double switchback maneuver. If the product worked, wouldn't you want to show the before and after pictures?

Krystal explained that the people in the photos were from a small village in Siberia where no one had ever used skin cream before. "Of course we pay them," she said with a shrug.

I was hardly listening. I was transfixed by the images of wrinkled-apple-faced ladies transformed into smooth-faced beauty queens.

Okay, the results weren't quite that dramatic. But they were dramatic enough. Enough that I couldn't stop thinking about how that skin cream might work on me.

I had to have it.

How Much?

The moment I was ready to talk numbers, though, Krystal wasn't. All of a sudden, Krystal wanted to talk about god.

"This morning I wake up and I pray to god," she said. "And god answered my prayers."

"Really?" For a moment, I was puzzled. If I were trying to sell face cream in Madison World I'm not sure I'd talk about god as a sales technique.

"I think you've been sent here for a reason," she said.

No kidding. If you are sitting in a chair with mysterious goop on your face you should know you have been sent there for a reason. And the reason is simple: They are going to extract money from you, one way or another. They can do it painfully or they can do it nicely. But either way, you are not going to get out of that chair, you are not going home, you will not pass go ever again until you open your pocketbook and let them pluck out a few thousand.

Again, I asked how much.

Again, Krystal tried to bamboozle me with the half of the two years and then two-thirds of the total math bullshit, but I told her to cut it out and give me the final number already. I began to get another very bad feeling when she refused to say the number out loud. When a person won't say a number out loud it's usually not good. It's what car salesmen do.

Instead, she wrote something down, circled it, and turned the pad around so I could see.

This time I didn't care how aged I looked. I leaned forward to squint at the numerals written on the pad.

They were blurry but I could make out a one, a five, and three zeros.

My mind couldn't take it in at first—15,000?

Fifteen thousand?

15K? Fifteen thousand dollars for face cream?

My heart began to beat in my lungs. I knew the face cream would be expensive but fifteen thousand dollars expensive? For a moment I felt as if I'd been shot into another universe.

I tried to explain to Krystal in the clearest way possible.

"I'm sorry. But I can't afford to spend fifteen thousand dollars on face cream."

"But it is really seventy-five hundred a year."

"I'm sorry. But I can't afford to spend *seventy-five hundred dollars a year* on face cream."

"But it is your face!" Krystal cried out, as if I were assailing the holy grail of womanhood. "It is what you present to the world. It is your passport to life."

The word "passport" reminded me of my most recent passport photo taken six months earlier. I looked shockingly bad.

Nevertheless, my resolve was stronger than a bad passport photo.

I sighed deeply. "I just can't."

Sensing something wasn't right, the older Russian guy strolled over.

"Is there a problem?" He looked from me to Krystal accusingly, as if we were both causing trouble in class. As if I weren't following the script and Krystal better get me back on board.

"Nope," I said, with a glance at Krystal. "No problem at all."

"Krystal is gonna change your life. You're gonna see. Whatever Krystal tell you to do, you'd better do it," he reminded me. And he shook his finger.

Krystal announced that it was time to remove the mask.

This was easier said than done. Getting the goop off was tedious and time-consuming.

Everyone in the store crowded around to see the results. Of course, there weren't any. But at that point, it didn't matter.

Fake Beauty

With the goop off my face, I knew it was my last chance to break free. If I let them put the goop on the other side I was stuck there for another half hour. Thirty minutes of saying nyet. There was no way I was going to run out into the street with a face full of goop.

They knew this as well.

And so, no matter what excuses I made, the Russians batted them away by pointing out that I couldn't possibly leave with one side of my face looking so much better than the other.

"I've got a good feeling about you," Krystal said. "I really do think you were sent here for a reason. I make up my mind. I'm going to help you."

"But—"

"You have a lot of friends, right?"

"Sure. I guess."

"I tell you what. You and I are going to make a deal."

I immediately seized on this as a possible way out of my dilemma. Even if I couldn't afford the face cream, certainly I had friends who could?

"Yes, I have lots of friends," I said. "And believe me, they're all going to want to buy this skin cream. I'll tell them about it, just as soon as I get out of here."

But Krystal wasn't going to go for that either. "You will tell your friends about the products. But not until I tell you to."

"Excuse me?"

"Tell no one. You must keep the secret of the cream. Keep quiet and wait until your friends mention your skin. Until they say, 'Hello, you look great. Your skin looks great.' Then, and only then, will you tell them the secret."

"Is this some kind of Facebook thing?"

"I predict it will happen in about three to four months."
She pulled her stool closer. "Tell me the truth. Is it really about the money?"

"Well . . ."

"How much do you spend on handbags?"

"I don't know." I felt like someone was sticking needles in my eyes.

"What about shoes? What if I said I could give you a two-year supply of products for ten pairs of shoes."

"No."

"You spend more money on your feet than your face? How long you gonna live like that?"

"I don't know."

"How about eight pairs of shoes?"

"Please," I cried out.

"Five?"

"I just can't."

"What can you pay then?" she demanded.

What could I say? Nothing? I can pay nothing? I looked around. Everyone in the store was staring at us.

"Maybe two and a half pairs?"

"That's not enough. How about . . ." Krystal wrote yet another number on the pad. She turned it around and held it up to my face.

"Yes?" she asked.

I looked at the number and gave up.

"Yes," I said. "Yes."

Face Cream Aftershock

My wallet was four thousand dollars lighter and my schlepping bags twenty pounds heavier as I left the store in shock. I was loaded down with products in different colored boxes. Inside the boxes were masks, ampules, creams, toners, cleansers, and scrubs, all of which came with instructions that included fuzzy photos of the products and the order in which to use them.

"So they got you," Queenie said when I returned to the Village that weekend.

"Yes, they did."

"How much?"

"Eeeee." I hedged. Could I tell her the truth? No. I couldn't even tell myself the truth. I couldn't digest it.

"Maybe two or three thousand?" I lied.

I couldn't explain it to myself. Was it possible that Krystal had somehow hypnotized me into spending all that money? Or was it just that I was too afraid to hurt her feelings or make her angry.

There was another part I didn't want to admit, and it was that I really wanted that face cream. But mostly, I really wanted that face cream *to work*.

I needed something to make sense. To not be a complete and utter waste of time.

Using the products wasn't easy. My routine involved doing drippy masks and having to lie down with slimy pads over my eyes. It meant scheduling time to take care of my skin.

But damn if that face cream didn't work and damn if it didn't happen exactly the way Krystal said it would.

For the first six weeks, no one noticed. But then I went to my dermatologist and he exclaimed that my rosacea had improved. After three months, my housekeeper insisted that I looked much younger and happier. After four months, I ran into old friends and they said they didn't recognize me I looked so youthful.

I knew the effects wouldn't last forever. The question was, what would I do when the cream ran out?

It happened sooner than expected. Just when my skin was at the peak of dewiness, three of the products ran out at once. And so I did what any sensible person would do and looked up the ingredients online and found other products that claimed to do the same thing and were much cheaper.

And then I didn't think about it, until finally, after the longest winter, the days began to warm up and the residents of Madison World came out, once again, into the sun.

And once again, the jewels glinted behind their plate glass windows while the mannequins sported outfits you could only wear in your imagination.

But not everything was the same. There were more dark places. Empty stores boarded up behind brown construction paper.

And so it was with a strange sort of relief that I discovered the Russians were still there on the stoop, harassing passersby.

I wondered if they would recognize me.

"Hey!" called out the Greek girl. "I really like your style."

I paused. Was this groundhog day?

Then I was annoyed. "Are you kidding me? Don't you remember? I came in here six months ago and got suckered into buying that face cream."

"You're one of our customers?" The girl looked at me as if she couldn't believe it. Was I not good enough for this store or just too wrinkled to be one of their clients? And then I got it. Maybe she couldn't believe I would be that stupid.

Here, she said, and pressed a sample packet of face cream into my hands.

I took it.

CHAPTER SIX

Middle-Aged Madness

"You won't believe what's happened," Tilda Tia said.

"Try me."

"You know how Ess and Jennifer went to that wellness retreat?"

"Uh-huh."

"Well, apparently they got into a big fight and Ess threw a drink in Jennifer's face."

I should have been surprised, but I wasn't.

Ess, fifty-three, and Jennifer, fifty-seven, are generally what are known as "nice" people. They rarely disagree with anyone and will happily sacrifice their feelings in order to prevent anyone else from feeling bad. In fact, they often go further, eager to take on blame for things that are clearly not their fault. These are the kind of women who watch *Real Housewives* and are sure it's completely made up.

But then something happens.

I call it middle-aged madness, or MAM.

MAM Strikes A Village

The weather might have partly been to blame. At eighty degrees, low humidity, and bright sunshine, it was the kind of weather that demanded gatherings and, of course, libations.

Indeed, it wasn't long before friends of friends began hearing about this fun time in the Village and began inviting themselves to stay. And that's when the trouble began.

First Sassy's friend Margo who had just decided to separate from her husband in Atlanta and was "trying out" single life went on a boating trip with a cub. Like most cub events, it lasted a lot longer than Margo expected, meaning she had a few too many drinks in the hot sun and got arrested in the parking lot of the marina when she tried to drive.

Then it spread to Marilyn.

Two months earlier Sassy and I could barely get Marilyn to leave her house. Now Marilyn wanted to go out. Every day and every night. She was at every party, invited or not. There was a flock of women from Europe staying in the Village with Queenie and soon they were all publicly removing their tops with San Tropez abandon.

The fights started when men began showing up. Kitty and Margo had words over a friend of Kitty's who was flirting with both of them. Marilyn and Queenie had words over something Marilyn said to Queenie's out-of-state boyfriend. Tilda Tia was having words with anyone who was willing to have words back.

And then Marilyn and I nearly came to blows.

There'd been a strange tension between me, Sassy, and Marilyn since the beginning of the summer that increased as the days got longer. Maybe because we'd never hung out in a pack of women before and Marilyn was playing to the crowd, but she began doing and saying things that felt curiously out of character. Having always insisted she was a behind-the-scenes kind of person, Marilyn became the center of attention, telling indiscrete stories about people and places that Sassy and I had never heard before. Of course, the women who'd just met Marilyn thought she'd always been like this.

It was impossible to explain that she hadn't and so, for a while, this before and after Marilyn caused a lot of confusion. One afternoon it came to a head, when Marilyn walked in to find me, Kitty, and Tilda Tia at the kitchen table. I don't remember the particulars of what set us off, but suddenly we were furious at each other.

I said, "I don't know who you are anymore."

She said, "This is who I am. This is the new me."

Then she grabbed her stuff and made to storm off.

"Don't you run away again the way you always do." I knew I sounded like an idiot because the truth was, Marilyn hadn't ever "run away" before because Marilyn and I had never had a confrontation.

And then the words came out like a slap.

"Fuck you!" Marilyn said.

I gasped. In twenty years of friendship, we'd never used the "F" word on each other. I couldn't believe it. What the hell was happening?

"How dare you!" I shouted, as we squared off in the dining room.

My heart was pumping in my stomach. This anger was deep and disturbing and atavistic, like I was confronting something evil that wasn't Marilyn. It seemed impossible that we could be this angry at each other. We raised our hands as if to strike.

We froze.

Something washed over us and we came to our senses.

I turned away and she turned away, or maybe it was the other way around. We separated. She out the front door and into her car and me back to Kitty's kitchen.

We each immediately called Sassy.

Sassy gave us a stern talking-to that we were grown women and we couldn't behave this way. This, she said, wasn't us.

She was right. It was MAM.

MAM vs. Midlife Crisis

On the surface, MAM resembles what people used to call a midlife crisis.

Years ago, this crisis happened mostly to men and mostly when they were around forty. It was considered a rite of passage, a railing against the restraints of society. Those fetters being the familial obligations and "the man" or the corporation where, once upon a time, most men worked. Back in the heyday of the male midlife crisis, a man would do stuff like buy a motorcycle or start reading *Playboy* or have an affair. Sometimes the midlife crisis led to divorce but not necessarily. It was considered a phase. Something that men went through.

Women, meanwhile, weren't allowed to have a midlife crisis. What they had instead were nervous breakdowns, which today we would call undiagnosed depression. And so, in the midlife crisis of old, while men ran around, women went to bed and pulled the covers over their heads.

Today, having a midlife crisis at fortysomething just sounds dumb. First of all, lots of people don't even find a partner and/or start having children until they're forty. At forty, people are finally beginning to grow up and behave sort of like adults. They buy places outside of big cities and have typical reproductive lifestyles that revolve around their children and the children-adjacent adults that children inevitably attract and that reproducers are invariably forced to call "friends."

Because today's reproductive lifestyle is so busy and exhausting and fraught, because it eats up so much psychic and emotional energy, it actually acts as a deterrent to a midlife crisis. There is simply no time to query the meaning of life or to ask the great question: Why am *I* here?

But just because the reproductive lifestyle pushes off a midlife crisis, it doesn't mean it goes away. It only means it happens later in life. Usually at a time when a midlife crisis couldn't be more inconvenient because a whole bunch of other major life-changing events—like divorce, death, moving, menopause, children leaving the nest, and the loss of a job—are happening as well.

It didn't used to be this way. At one time, fiftysomething meant the beginning of retirement—working less, slowing down, spending more time on hobbies and with your friends, who, like you, were sliding into a more leisurely lifestyle. In short, retirement-age folk weren't expected to do much of anything except get older and a bit fatter and to need to go to the doctor and the bathroom more. They weren't expected to exercise, start new business ventures, move to a different state, have casual sex with strangers, get arrested, and start all over again, except with one-tenth of the resources and in many cases going back to the same social and economic situation that they spent all of their thirties and forties trying to crawl out of.

But this is exactly what the lives of a lot of fifty- and sixty-something women now look like today.

The Exploding Breast Implant and the Happily Unhappily Ever After Story

Take Ess. In many ways, her story is typical of a woman in MAM, with the exception that her MAM story takes place in the cushioned world of the 1 percent. Meaning, theoretically, Ess should always be able to afford a roof over her head.

Ess is not a paragon of female virtue, nor is she meant to be. She's a representation of a certain kind of woman who does what society tells women they should do, who wants what society tells women they should want, and who's found it's best not to think too deeply about it.

Ess grew up in Southern New England in a large ranch house in a development of new houses. It was one of those places where everyone makes relatively the same income and enjoys a similar lifestyle and dresses in a similar manner, in clothing from the same outlet stores and catalogues.

Ess had two older brothers and a younger sister. Ess and one brother, Jimmy, got the looks. Her sister, who looked exactly like her mother, was considered the smart one. Ess was Daddy's little girl. Like a lot of men in those days, Ess's father was what would now be considered an alcoholic but back then was considered an "everyday drinker." He returned from the office at five and threw back three G&Ts by the time Ess's mother tried to make everyone sit down for dinner at six. Sometimes Dad's drinking was a good thing. Sometimes not so good. When it wasn't so good, Ess figured out that by amusing and entertaining her father she could jolly him out of his terrible mood and everyone in the family was silently grateful. This she figured out, was her job. Probably for life.

When she graduated from high school, Ess assessed her cards. She was tall and slim, with a figure that was labeled "athletic," a euphemism for flat chested. Ess was a solid A cup.

This was a major bummer. Being flat chested was on the very top of the list of egregious female imperfections, above "fat," "hairy," and "fat and hairy." Being flat chested was considered an abnormality, an insult to the male gender, the facts of which her brothers never tired of reminding her. They weren't the only ones. All through tenth grade she'd been bullied by one particular boy about her lack of plentitude. He used to drive by her house on his motorcycle and shoot at her with his BB gun.

"Someday I'm gonna kill you," he'd shout.

"It's because he likes you and he doesn't know how to express it," her mother said, although Ess knew this was a lie. He really did hate her.

And as she looked at herself in the mirror, Ess realized there was a way to get revenge on that boy and all the others like him: become a model.

She succeeded. She worked a lot, enough to support herself in the world of money, drugs, and rock 'n' roll where models could spend their time when they weren't in front of the camera. Unlike a lot of other girls, though, Ess never expected that lifestyle was going to be her life. She wanted the kind of loving, rough-and-tumble family she'd had as a kid.

At twenty-five, Ess married the love of her life, a handsome, former professional soccer player from Ireland who'd transitioned into working in commercial real estate. It was considered an auspicious pairing. Ess was a social dynamo—the kind of person who knew how to oil the water between strangers, who could draw out an intimate confession from the most powerful man in the room. She was a woman who was a fixer, a woman who wasn't dangerous. A woman who liked to help you solve your problems. Her husband, meanwhile, with his sports background, impressed all her relatives at their Fourth of July barbeques.

The marriage was good for about five years and then real life rushed in.

Ess had two boys. They moved out of New York and her husband lost his contacts and made less money and she tried to work but the only thing she'd ever made money at was modeling and there was no way she was ever going to have the body to do it again. The situation continued for another few years, and then her husband, now in his early forties, had *his* midlife crisis and ran away.

It turned out her husband had no money. It was an easy divorce because there was nothing to split up.

With nowhere else to go, Ess moved back home, back to the ranch house where she'd grown up. Except this time, it was her sons in her brothers' bedrooms and herself in her frilly pink childhood bed.

Her parents loved their grandchildren. But they were in their seventies, smack in the middle of what was once a typical retirement that included several hours of golf each day and weekend getaways to Mohegan Sun where they went to see Celine Dion. A divorced forty-two-year-old daughter and her two sons living at home was not their idea of what their life should look like.

If this were a made-up story, this is the part where Ess would determine to change. She would stop letting life happen *to* her and *take actions* that would enable her to write her own narrative. She would find a place to live for her and her two nearly teenage boys that was small but clean and fix-up-able and she would paint the walls herself and would magically get her boys to help her. When they threw paint at each other and laughed, we'd know that Ess was going to turn this boat around. That she was going to find a job at a bakery where she would discover a secret talent for cake decoration—and all would be fine. In the stories women tell each other, the woman always has some special skill or unfound "gift" that allows her to make money, take care of herself and her children, and keep her dignity.

Real life, however, doesn't always work that way.

In the mirror of her childhood bedroom, Ess once again summed up her assets: Her face still looked good. Her legs still looked good. But her breasts—her goddamned breasts again—they looked bad. Two flesh sacks in the shape of torpedoes. Against her mother's warnings—"small breasts don't recover from breastfeeding" she'd hissed every time Ess had unbuttoned her shirt—Ess had breastfed. She'd wanted to protect her boys from damage, only to discover there were no defenses against life's random bad luck.

In the old world, the world where people stayed together, sagging breasts and outward signs of aging didn't matter. But back in this world they did.

Hence Ess's visit to the breast surgeon.

Ess got his name from one of her friends and when she went in, she was surprised to find that he was a stumpy, ordinary-looking fellow who reminded her of someone's father. He wore an optical mask over his face that obscured his eyes and made him resemble a robot.

The nurse, who was in the room the whole time, gently pulled the paper gown below Ess's shoulders to reveal the lifeless flesh. Looking away, the surgeon carefully handled her breasts as if he were weighing counters in his hands.

He slid back on his stool and sighed. She straightened, quickly pulling up the gown.

"I think I can make you very, very happy," he said.

"You can?"

"I can make you a D cup. Maybe even a double D. You've got lots of extra flesh."

"Is that good?" she asked.

"It's terrific," the nurse nodded. "It means they can be bikini-model big."

"Like a twenty-one-year-old," the doctor said proudly.

Luckily, Ess wanted to look like a twenty-one-year-old. Otherwise the whole thing would have creeped her out.

She had to pay for the procedure up front: thirty-five hundred dollars put on her credit card.

She awoke from the operation to what she was told was more good news: "Doctor was able to make you just a bit larger. You're now officially an E cup!" the nurse squealed, so that "E cup" came out like the sound a mouse might make. "Isn't that fantastic?"

Ess tried to take a deep breath and nearly panicked. There was an unfamiliar weight on her chest. The weight of breasts. Of sexiness. Of desire and of being desired. For a moment, she wondered what she'd done. Was she ready for this? She could tell the breasts were big from the weight. She wondered how she was going to maneuver these saline receptacles through the world—literally. Her breasts would be unavoidable, and everyone would look at them. The thought of men looking at her, of desiring her, turned her on again.

"You're going to have so much fun in your new body. Shopping, buying bras," the nurse waxed on. "And now you have the perfect excuse to buy yourself a whole new wardrobe. You'll see. Your entire life is going to change."

She looked wistful and why not? All women are familiar with the story of the makeover journey. Indeed, we relish it as a success story. If a woman can make herself over into a more pleasing, commercial, universally acceptable version of a stereotypical female, she *can live an entirely different life.*

Indeed, Ess discovered that having this new body was almost like having a baby. Everyone was celebrating. But this time around she wasn't tired and she looked amazing and she could drink. It wasn't long before she'd made some new girlfriends. She met them at happy hour at a bar on the pier near the train station. Some of them were married, some weren't, but they were all tanned and groomed and wore expensive clothes and, like her, had breast implants.

Suffocating under the tacit disapproval of her parents, Ess took to leaving the house to cut loose with her new friends, who were sympathetic to her tale of woe. How she'd married the love of her life and he'd destroyed her and now she was going to do what she should have done in the beginning. She was going to marry a man for money.

Outwardly, her friends applauded her. In the world of women, using a man for his money is payback for men using women for, well, just about everything.

Nevertheless, while the *idea* of marrying a man for his money seems like a good one, the actual execution of it often proves vexing. Finding a man at all, even if he has an equal amount of money, is hard enough. In other words, when a woman says, "I'm going to find a rich man to marry," most women are secretly thinking, "Yeah, right."

But Ess said it and did it. And that's what makes her story a bit different.

She also admitted that she wasn't in love with the man, right up until her wedding day. This was also unusual. In the story of marrying a man for his money, the woman isn't supposed to admit it. She's supposed to at least pretend to love the guy. But Ess didn't do that. As she got dressed in the ornate bridal suite in the thousand-dollar-a-night destination hotel, surrounded by her bridesmaids, Ess reminded everyone that she was only marrying Eddie for his dough.

"Then don't do it, sweetie," begged a couple of her friends.

"I have to. For my sons. Well, ladies," she said as they lifted the bridal dress over her raised arms, "here goes nothing."

For the next five years, even though her husband, Eddie, was mean-spirited and selfish, never seeming to tire of telling her and other people how stupid she was, Ess didn't complain. Her boys had a fine roof over their heads, and they had the best schooling, and that was what mattered. And when her husband began to drink more and occasionally became violent, she brushed it off. She'd made her bed and would lie in it and make the best of it even if she had to do it for the rest of her life.

And then her husband went to the doctor and the doctor told him if he didn't stop smoking cigars and drinking, he would die.

Some men would have brushed this off—after all, everyone is going to die "someday"—but not Eddie. He was one of those middle-aged men who suddenly see the light and run right into it.

Eddie returned from his doctor's visit white and shaken. Ess was in the kitchen, mixing up a batch of white fruit sangria. When Ess saw Eddie's pale, sweaty face, for a moment she thought he was having a heart attack, and for a moment her initial reaction was not one of fear or terror but of joy that perhaps her husband was going to die and solve all their problems. But life was not that kind.

"I'm scared," Eddie said.

He immediately went on what was once known as a health kick.

This happens when a person who always had very little interest in their body suddenly becomes obsessed. They take up exercise and everything that goes with it, like gadgets to measure their progress and count calories. And one by one, they begin giving things up: carbs, sugar, gluten, wheat, meat, and dairy. And, of course, alcohol.

Back in the day, when this happened, everyone would kind of shake their heads and keep right on drinking that cocktail. Excessive interest in one's health was considered self-indulgent. You weren't supposed to try to cheat god of his moment to decide when your time was up by trying to lengthen your life through exercise. Indeed, a sudden interest in one's health was usually a sign that death wasn't far behind. You could run as fast as you could, but death still caught up with you, as illustrated by the fact that it was common for middle-aged men to suddenly drop dead of a heart attack while running.

That night, while Ess drank white sangria, she and Eddie got into a nasty fight. Eddie insisted that since he had to stop drinking, she had to stop drinking as well. She also needed to give up meat and carbs. When she objected, he told her she'd become fat and didn't take care of herself and didn't turn him on anymore. The next morning, Eddie stormed off to Miami where he checked himself into a seventy-thousand-dollar-a-month rehab facility.

It worked. Sort of. Eddie returned sober, ten pounds lighter, obsessed with yoga and krav maga and kale. He also wanted a divorce.

He left the house and went to stay at a fancy hotel.

Ess began innocently nosing through his things. It wasn't long before she found something: Yes, Eddie had gone to rehab for a month. But immediately afterward he'd gone to a hotel and paid thousands of dollars for transactional sex with a variety of women.

Ess reached out to her girlfriends, who rushed to her side.

More sordid details came out. How Eddie had once been so drunk he'd passed out on a plane and peed himself. How he had thrown a friend's skis off the gondola because she asked him to put out his cigar. How he'd called Ess fat.

Clearly, Eddie was the villain.

Like many men, however, the ability to look at one's sexist and abusive behavior and see anything wrong with it eluded Eddie. And yet, being a man, there had to be a winner and a loser. Since he could not be the loser, he had to try to be the winner. Which meant Ess must be demonized. Ess must be shown that it was all her fault.

Eddie hired an attack-dog superlawyer and put him on to Ess. The superlawyer claimed that he'd heard Ess was telling people that Eddie was a bully, an abuser, and alcoholic, and now Eddie was going to sue her for slander on top of divorcing her.

This new and unpleasant chest-thumping male in Ess's life caused her very high levels of stress and anxiety. Each communication put her into a red-level fight-or-flight mode. She was practically bursting with cortisol.

In fact, all that stress might have caused what happened next: one of Ess's breast implants exploded.

Tilda Tia pointed out that this wasn't actually surprising. She said that breast implants often went wrong, and they didn't last forever, although they usually didn't tell you that before they put them in.

And so, in the middle of this terrible divorce, Ess went into the hospital for the first of a two-part operation to remove the implant. When she awoke her chest was covered with slightly bloody crisscrossed bandages.

She didn't feel terrible though. Not terrible enough to resist tempting fate by laughing at her situation and asking, "What else can go wrong, right?"

If Ess were in any other time phase, this would have been a rhetorical question. But because Ess was in a MAM cycle, the answer to "what else can go wrong?" was "just you wait."

On the third day of her recovery, Ess got a phone call from her brother informing her that her eighty-seven-year-old father had been out driving and hit a tree. He'd been taken to the hospital and pronounced dead fifteen minutes before.

And as far as her brothers and her mother were concerned, it was all Ess's fault.

Ess had taken on the responsibility of her parents, checking in on them regularly and driving her father to the store or wherever else he wanted to go—often to the local diner—where they'd order bad-for-you sandwiches piled with processed meats and cheeses. But that ended when Ess became embroiled in her divorce and her medical emergency. Which was also her fault. She'd finally found a rich man, someone who could take care of her. And now she'd blown it. Couldn't she do anything right?

Ess began having bad MAM thoughts.

Bad MAM Moments

There are psychic moments in MAM that will make you want to scream. When you'll stare in the mirror and see no reason for going on, when you'll have a day that's just like a black hole.

Thoughts are like little feet. They start making a path that then becomes a trough of self-doubt and despair. What did I do to deserve this? Where did I go wrong? And: *Is this really my life?*

That began to happen to Ess. Now, when she woke up, she started to think that maybe it would be better—for herself and everyone else—if she didn't.

But then she'd realize she was being silly and self-indulgent. She had her sons to think about. And the second operation to look forward to.

And here, lady luck had finally tapped her magic wand. Because the implant had exploded, insurance would also cover the reconstruction, requiring liposuction and a small tummy tuck. In short, Ess's body would be surgically reshaped.

Ess took care in packing for the operation. She knew what to expect from her last visit. The constant beeping. The hazy, twilight sleep. The polyester hospital linens. The nice people on staff who were, when she thought about it, the only people who had been nice to her in the last six weeks. Who at least bothered to pretend to care and therefore perhaps did?

Was such a thing possible?

As Ess drove herself to the hospital, she realized she was looking forward to her stay.

The next morning, wrapped like a mummy in a tight girdle, support bra, and a gel sports wrap that was the latest technology in bandages, Ess returned home.

She went through the heavy front door, through the double-height foyer—a requirement in the homes of the affluent, as if there is no greater sign of money than needless headspace—and went up one of the double staircases and into the master suite with its walk-in closet and hall of mirrors. She held out her cell phone. She took a picture.

She sent it to five of her friends. Then she got into bed and slept for sixteen hours.

One of those friends was Tilda Tia. She reported that the operation was a huge success and you couldn't believe how amazing Ess looked.

She showed us the most recent photos. Wearing black athletic wear over the support garments, Ess appeared to have shed half her body weight.

"I can't believe they can do that," I said.

"It's incredible what they can do these days," Tilda Tia said. "And thank god. Now at least maybe she can find another man. Because let's face it. She doesn't have a lot of options. It's not like she can get a job."

I blanched.

"It's a reality," Tilda Tia said scoldingly. "Not every woman has a big career. Look at Jerry Hall. She married an eighty-seven-year-old man. That's what's out there if you're a woman like Ess."

"Except it's a much lesser version," Kitty pointed out. "Which is even more depressing."

Nevertheless, we all agreed the surgery was a triumph. Every friend's triumph, no matter how they get there, is a triumph for all. It shows that maybe we can do what we're all afraid we can't: beat the odds.

But MAM doesn't work that way.

MAM is like Medusa—cut off one head and two grow back.

Two weeks later, while Ess was still at home recuperating, she got a call from her old friend Jennifer. She and Jennifer hadn't seen each other for years, but Jen had heard about Ess's situation and wanted to see how she was. Ess was grateful. She filled Jennifer in on her latest batch of troubles. She'd had to put the house on the market and Eddie had told the real estate agent she was an alcoholic. She missed her father terribly and her mother was still not speaking to her and wouldn't let her have any of her father's things. And her boys were away at camp and she was all alone.

Jennifer suggested if not actually a solution, at least a break from her problems—a trip to a spa in Arizona. Jennifer had won the trip for two in a raffle. All Ess would need to pay for was her flight.

Ess said yes. And it might have been just what she needed if MAM wasn't about to light up the sky with stink bombs.

Because in MAM, two women who once thought they had everything in common can suddenly discover their lives couldn't be more different.

Like Ess, Jennifer also had two children and had been married twice. At the beginning of her career as a real estate agent, Jen had met a perfectly fine man. They'd married and had two daughters, while Jennifer continued to work.

By the time they were in their early thirties, they both cheated and the marriage fell apart. But unlike Ess's situation, when her first husband left, Jennifer didn't have to sell the house. In fact, she didn't have to move or change her life at all. In a sense, she had it easy. Her life went on pretty much the same as before, with her working and taking care of her girls and the house, except that her husband was no longer in the picture.

Eventually Jennifer met a wonderful man who was her age and also a real estate agent and they married and started their own firm together.

Now, fifteen years later, they're still together. They live in a very nice house and they have savings and lots of friends. Jen is close to her daughters, who live nearby. And soon, Jen knows, like her, her daughters will meet someone nice in their circle. They'll marry, have children, and also work. Jennifer is her daughters' role model.

At one time, Ess thought her life—although perhaps not quite as happy—would end up resembling Jennifer's.

Now it wouldn't. A fact neither one would realize until they clashed in Arizona.

Jennifer, who was traveling from a different airport, got up early to do a yoga class before her flight. Ess, meanwhile, woke up late and flustered. She'd been drinking too much and doing some of it alone. In the past, drinking would have eased the pain, and usually when she woke up, everything was generally okay. Now that was no longer true. She drank, she woke up, and something else was wrong again. Like her passport was about to expire.

But she noticed something different as she walked through the airport. People weren't casting their eyes away at the sight of her the way they had before the surgery. It had to be her new body. She smiled at one or two, and when they smiled back, she began to think that this trip was going to be the perfect tonic for the lousy last few months.

Ess made her way to the bar. She and the bartender immediately got into a conversation and she found out everything about his life and how he lived an hour from the airport and had to get up every morning at 5:00 a.m. He ended up giving her two free drinks and she gave him a forty-dollar tip she couldn't afford.

On the plane, Ess made more new friends. A woman and three men. They had a jolly time and the people around them didn't mind when they got a bit too loud. The passengers were either going on vacation or going home, heading to people and places they looked forward to seeing.

Ess landed in Arizona with the sickening thud that happens when all the alcohol you've consumed on the flight coagulates into a roaring hangover in regular atmosphere. There was only one way to combat it: with a small sip of something.

She went to a bar, ordered a glass of red wine, and picked up her phone. She had four texts from Jennifer.

Where are you? Are you okay?

The texts annoyed her. She wanted to write back: *What are you, my mother?*

Just landed, she wrote. She chugged down the glass of wine, partly in defiance.

✻　✻　✻

Outside the revolving door, the heat was dry and heavy.

"Hiiiiii," Jennifer said. She was waiting just outside, glancing from her phone to the exit. "Oh my god," she exclaimed. "You look amazing."

"Thank you," Ess said. "I feel amazing."

"Well, wow," Jen said.

"You look great," Ess said.

Jen gave a modest head drop to the side. It was her trademark gesture when people told her how good she looked. Jen was beautiful and she'd never gained a pound and she hadn't had plastic surgery and yet she looked at least fifteen years younger, thanks to her careful years of clean living. She was also an incredibly nice person, as if she knew she'd been blessed with these great looks but it wasn't important to her. She was annoying, Ess remembered. That might have been one of the reasons they didn't end up being the bestest of friends. Jen's very control of her physical self was a sort of rebuke to others. If she could do it, why couldn't you?

During the ride, the driver extolled the beauty of the Arizona landscape. They passed small, crumbling ranch houses with pokey horses in pens, then orange stucco developments, acres and acres of them reaching to the bottom of the mountains and then strip mall after strip mall until they came to an area where there were trees and green grass and sprinklers and upscale chain restaurants.

But when the car pulled into the entrance, Ess's mood plummeted. It was so barren and concrete. Not at all what she'd been expecting.

The people at the ranch were smiling, though, and nice, like the people at the hospital. Here they all wore light-blue uniforms accented with a darker hue. This should have worked, but there was something off about the shades of blue. Instead of going together, they clashed.

The fact that she'd noticed reminded Ess of how out of place she felt.

But then the guy who took their luggage began joking and perhaps even flirting with her, and Ess remembered why she was here: to have fun.

She made a point of saying it out loud to the head thera-pists who asked them what their goals were for their stay. "I'm here to have fun!" Ess declared. This made the therapists smile and nod at each other in approval.

"I'm here to have fun, too," Jennifer said.

As you can imagine, the two women's ideas of fun were vastly different.

For the first two hours, Ess tried her best. There weren't treatments in the afternoon, so she and Jen sat out by the pool centered in an expanse of cement painted in swirly col-ors. Nearby was a vending machine selling healthy snacks.

Jennifer pulled out a few small bills from her designer wallet and fed them into the machine. "Here." She handed Ess a package of rice and dried tofu creations.

They lay down on chaises on either side of an umbrella.

"So," Jen said. She pulled at the fluted cellophane containing raw pumpkin seeds. The seam gave way and a few seeds exploded onto Jen's oiled belly. She carefully picked them up and placed them in a napkin. "So," she repeated. "Tell me everything."

Ess began. But maybe because there was no alcohol, Jen didn't seem as interested as she would have in the past. In the past, she'd have been excited about Ess's relationship trauma. In the past, nothing was more interesting and important than relationship trauma.

"Oh, Ess. I'm sorry," Jen said.

"I know. It's boring," Ess said. "I mean, what did I expect? I never loved him."

Jen nodded. She picked up the napkin with the seeds in it and got up to deposit it in a trash container stained with spilled iced tea.

"You know," she began when she returned. "It might be that it wasn't all Eddie's fault."

"What do you mean?" Ess was immediately on high alert.

Jen considered. What did she mean? What she wanted to say was that if Ess could admit to her duplicity in the situation—she did drink a bit too much, and she shouldn't have married Eddie in the first place, and she needed to stop living her life relying on men—then perhaps she could learn from it. And become a better person.

But Jen realized that now was not the time. Instead, she became soothing. "I didn't mean anything. Only that when I got divorced, I really had to take a look at myself and how I was to blame for some of it."

Ess's eyes narrowed. "Yes," she said. "But that was over twenty years ago. And you cheated on your husband. And he caught you."

"I just meant—" Jen broke off.

"I know, I know," Ess said. "I'm tense. Maybe I need to lie down."

They agreed to part ways for a nap.

Ess went into her room. She lay down on the bed, but it was hard and after five minutes she was bored with her own company. She checked her phone. Two of the guys from the plane had texted.

One was staying in a hotel. The other one was at his house, which wasn't far away.

Ess texted him back and told him to pick her up at the gates of the spa and they'd go get a drink.

They went to a TGI Friday's.

Ess had forgotten how good that food was, nachos with cheese and those fat canned jalapeños on top. She drank a few margaritas. She became drunk. It wasn't necessarily a pleasant feeling.

She asked if the guy could drive her back to the spa.

He could. In fact, he seemed relieved to be rid of her. He dropped her by a side door.

Ess went up the outside stairs. She thought she was on the second floor, but it turned out she was on the third floor. She didn't know that though until she tried to open what she thought was her door and a woman in a bathrobe with goop on her face answered and said, "Honey, you're lost." And then Ess, like a goat that has no idea where to go, went down an elevator and over a glassed-in bridge that bisected the lobby. The woman at the front desk saw her and waved frantically, but Ess found another set of stairs and began climbing. She went down a long hallway, turning left three times. The fourth time she ran right into Jen, who was standing in the hall. She was in her robe and hotel slippers with a security guard by her side. "I'll take things from here," she said, pushing open the door to Ess's room after the security guard unlocked it.

"Oh sweetie," Jen said. She pulled back the covers on the bed and shook her head. "What am I going to do with you?"

"I'm sorry," Ess called out gaily and waved her hand. Flapped it rather, like a bird with a broken wing.

"How are you feeling?" asked the head therapist the next morning. She put her moisturized hand on top of Ess's shoulder and leaned in. "If you need to talk about your problem, I'm here."

"I'm fine," Ess insisted.

She was fine. She was hungover. Big deal.

Except somehow, it was.

It was the spa itself that was to blame Ess decided. Who could feel better in this bleak temple of health?

No one. And so Ess came up with a plan.

All afternoon she went about recruiting other women, from the line in the cafeteria to the steam room to the yoga mats, where women like her, who hadn't exercised in a million years, struggled to hold the positions. Like Ess, it turned out that they, too, wanted to have fun. Like Ess, they, too, wanted to relive those youthful days when friendship meant going out to eat, drink, and be merry.

Jen was a different story. It took a bit of work to convince her, but she finally relented, acknowledging that once upon a time she, too, had been one of those eat, drink, and be merry women.

And so a group of six women went to a local place where there was old-fashioned line dancing. In the center was a dance floor ringed with picnic tables. There were guys in authentic cowboy gear. It had the feel of a tourist spot except it was real.

They settled at an empty table. A harried server nodded her head at them as she spun away. "I'm going to order drinks at the bar," Ess said, getting up.

"I'll come with you." Jennifer took Ess's arm. She glanced back at the women they'd left at the table.

"What are we doing here?"

"What do you mean? It's fun."

"Well," Jen said.

"Look at those guys," Ess said, indicating two men straight ahead. They were large, good old boy types. "Hot," Ess declared.

"Who?" Jen looked around then frowned in disbelief. "Them? Those guys? They are not hot."

Ess went over and started talking to them.

In Jen's telling, it just got worse from there. Ess started dancing. She got some woman to trade shoes with her. And then she might have found someone to give her some kind of drug.

And that's when it happened. The incident.

Ess was propping herself up at the bar. While the muscles in her face were moving they had bypassed what could be considered normal expressions.

Jen was triggered. By all kinds of things. Memories of the two of them twenty-five years ago. But mostly what set her off was that Ess was stumbling and incoherent and once again Jen was going to have to take care of her and mother her. Get her to put down her drink and come outside and maybe she wouldn't have to stop in the bathroom first.

And hopefully she wouldn't puke.

Another mess to clean up.

"Ess!" Jen said. She said it more forcefully and maybe more disgustedly than she should have, but she was pissed. Nevertheless, her tone was what got Ess's attention.

Ess immediately went on the defensive, demanding to know what was wrong with Jen.

Jen sighed. She knew she shouldn't have spoken harshly. The more ramped up Ess got, the harder it would be to get her out of there. Which Jen, in her near sobriety, saw clearly was now her only mission, whether she liked it or not.

She dropped her tone. "Come on, sweetie," she said.

Ess dropped the façade as well and became overly jolly. "Come over here and meet K," she said, indicating the guy.

Jen gave him her side head and said formally, "Nice to meet you. If you don't mind, we've got to go."

"Maybe *you've* got to go," the guy said.

Jen looked at him dumbfounded. The men she knew didn't speak to women like that. He couldn't be serious.

"Excuse me?"

"Take a ride. Cash it outside. Me and your friend are having fun getting to know each other so why don't you take off."

"Why don't you take off," Jen snapped. The rush of anger felt good.

She turned back to Ess. "Let's go."

"No," Ess said.

Jen looked around in frustration. She put her hands on her hips. "Ess. Please."

Jen was sure she saw Ess's eyes flash just before she shouted, "Shut the fuck up!" And then her arm shot forward and a Frisbee-shaped puddle of beer struck Jen on the side of the face.

The force of it knocked her head like a bobblehead doll. When her head snapped back, she realized her hair was wet along with half of her face. Panicked, she put her hands on her hair and when they came away, she almost expected to see blood.

Instead it was only thin, foamy, piss-colored beer.

"Oh my god," Ess said and folded her hands over her mouth.

Jen suspected she was laughing.

She grabbed a handful of napkins, patted herself down as best she could, and took a taxi back to the spa.

Showered and back in her bathrobe, Jen thought about sending Ess a long email telling her what she really thought of her. But she was too charged up. Then she called her husband and told him the story and cried. He told her to forget about it. That made her angry and so she unloaded on him about what a terrible person Ess was and her nice husband, who'd always liked Ess, was forced to concede that yes, he'd known there was something deeply wrong with Ess all along.

"Et tu, Ess," he whispered.

Ess stayed at the cowboy place for another hour. The women from the spa had all disappeared, and so had the guy who'd caused the ruckus.

She went out to the parking lot. She went behind a lamp-post and cried for a little bit, but then she saw a cop and he called a taxi for her.

The next morning, Ess took the first flight out. She didn't talk to Jen. She didn't talk to anyone.

She had a drink at the bar before her flight and passed out nearly as soon as they closed the doors.

It was early evening by the time Ess got home. Coming upon her house after a turn in the road, Ess was thrilled to see the familiar driveway and the pink-blooming magnolia tree where her dogs loved to lie on a summer afternoon. And there was the house itself. Somehow she'd forgotten how grand it was. And how when she'd first moved in with her boys, she'd thought she was the luckiest woman in the world.

Back then, when she thought about her future, she vaguely envisioned Eddie dying before her and leaving her everything, including the house, where she would live out her latter days in peace.

She knew now that wouldn't be true.

It was really all she knew.

Moving on from MAM

Eventually, Ess would figure it out. Most women do. Moving on from MAM means taking a good look at the reality of your life and discovering what you can build from it. A good example of this was Sassy's friend, Margo.

Like most women who experience MAM, Margo never expected to find herself in the position she was in: nearly sixty, single, and without a permanent place to live, with no income coming in and no job or career. At some point in the hazy future, she would get some money, when her soon-to-be ex-husband in Atlanta sold their house.

Margo hadn't had a regular job in twenty years, but she did have a talent. She could paint, and people were impressed with her paintings. Sassy and I each bought one and so did a few other friends, and this, we thought, could solve Margo's money problems. We were sure a local gallery would discover her. They would start selling her paintings for ten, twenty, fifty thousand dollars and Margo would be saved. Surely, there were enough rich people in the vicinity for whom fifty thousand dollars was the equivalent of fifty dollars for everyone else?

Of course, the reality was very different. Margo packed her paintings into the back of her Jeep and drove them around to galleries. She found one that could sell her paintings for twelve hundred dollars. Margo had to pay for the framing, however, which was expensive. After the gallery took their cut, she could expect to clear five hundred dollars. The store guessed that they would sell one or two paintings a month, which would add up to one thousand dollars. Not quite enough to live on in a place where the cheapest rent was at least two thousand a month.

And so, that winter we worried. Not just about Margo but also about Queenie, who had had a couple of fainting spells. And about Marilyn, who was back to hiding in her house.

There were no guarantees. While we'd sit around the fire at night, it didn't escape us that while Margo had done everything that was once considered "right"—she'd worked, married, had children, and then she'd pulled back and out of the income stream in order to stay home, take care of the kids, and perform all the other endless duties of the reproductive lifestyle—it had left her with nothing. Meanwhile, Sassy and I, who had bucked the family tradition, were okay. We had houses and retirement plans and savings in the bank.

Margo didn't. She needed a job.

Three months later she found one: measuring blinds for a decorating firm that did houses for the very rich.

It paid fifteen dollars an hour for forty hours a week. That was six hundred a week, twenty-four hundred a month, nearly twenty-nine thousand a year, not including taxes, which was nearly the same salary she'd been making thirty-five years ago back in the early 1980s. Back in a different century.

But it had health insurance. That was the good part.

It was also a job she knew well. It had been her first job back when she was twenty-two and working for a famous decorator on the Upper East Side. It had been exciting back then. She was just starting out, convinced it was all going to work out for her.

Now, nearly forty years later, she'd come full circle.

Or she would have, if MAM hadn't decided to give her one more chance.

At 8:00 a.m. on the morning that Margo was supposed to start her first day of work, the phone rang.

"Hello?"

"Margo?" It was her brother. "Aunt Penny died."

Good old Aunt Penny. Margo's father's sister. She'd never married and had no children and had left all her money to Margo and her brother.

And because Aunt Penny had always worked, she had quite a substantial IRA built up.

And so Margo was saved! At least in the sense that she didn't have to take the job measuring blinds.

"A miracle," Sassy declared.

We all agreed that this was the result of Margo's good karma. Of always being nice and being there for other people and look—the universe had finally decided to be there for her.

Sort of. The money was just enough to afford her a small house in a rural area where it's a twenty-minute drive to the supermarket.

Margo doesn't mind. She says the solitude is worth it to pursue her dream of painting full time.

Still, sometimes I worry about Margo. I ask Sassy questions. Is she lonely up there? Who does she see? Who does she hang out with?

I wonder if she's disappointed with her life, the way I sometimes am. And if she worries about the price she'll pay for being a woman in the first place and not doing everything right, the way I often do. And then I calm myself with the mantra that has soothed women for ages when we ask those questions: It's all about choices. Like we actually have control over our lives.

CHAPTER SEVEN

A Boy and His Father: An Adventure in Adjacent Mothering

THE BOY and his father arrived in the middle of a heat wave.

Inside my house, where I barely had air-conditioning, I took a deep breath and reminded myself not to be annoyed. Not to be angry. Not to be upset that Max promised—promised—that he and the boy would be here by two.

It was now six.

The phone rang and I grabbed it. Sassy. "Are they there yet?" she asked.

"No," I said, between gritted teeth. "They only left the city an hour ago."

"But I thought they were supposed to leave the city in the morning."

"They were. But the tents didn't arrive."

"What?"

"The tents. I found out this morning that Max ordered them online *last night*. Who does that? Who orders online at the last minute? He's known they were coming for weeks."

"Honey. It's called being a man," Sassy reassured me. "If it gets too difficult, you can take them to Kitty's. And Queenie's. We'll all help."

"Thank you." I exhaled gratefully.

"What's the son's name again?"

I froze. "Something Icelandic?"

"You don't know?" she asked incredulously.

"I can't remember," I said. They hadn't even arrived and already I felt like a loser for not remembering the kid's name. "He's only eight and he barely speaks English," I added by way of an excuse. "But I'm sure it will all be fine."

"It will all be fine" was my new mantra. MAM had moved on and I was in a good place. I was doing the stuff they always tell middle-aged people to do. I was "staying active," "eating healthy," and I wasn't drinking "too much." I always made sure to fill up my rosé glass with ice. And I was working. Five to six hours a day, from eight till two.

I was happy. I was calm.

And so, when one of my ex-boyfriends—let's call him Max—called me up and asked if he and his son could camp in the backyard of my house in the Village for ten days, I agreed.

The kid was dying to go camping and Max had promised he would take him. The kid wanted to be near the woods to see animals in the night. The kid wanted to catch his own fish and eat it. The kid wanted to sleep in a tent.

My yard was big enough to provide all that, I pointed out. I even had what could be considered a "cabin"—the old barn in my backyard. It had a newly poured cement floor and electricity. Never mind that it really was a barn that flooded when it rained. What kid wouldn't want to stay there?

I was sure I could handle the visit. I'd stick to my routine of working every morning while Max spent bonding time with his son. There was one snag: Max didn't drive. He didn't have a license and hadn't had one for over thirty years, being one of those people who have always lived in cities and is used to taking public transport.

"No problem," I exclaimed. "You don't need a car in the Village. You can ride bikes everywhere. How old is the boy again?"

"Eight," the father said. We agreed this was old enough, certainly, to be proficient on a bike?

We made a plan. One that, as usual, I pushed to the back of my mind and didn't think about until the appointed day was less than a week away.

"Are they actually coming?" Sassy asked.

I shrugged. "Who knows? You know Max. He might change his mind at the last minute."

Max had a very laissez-faire attitude toward the rules of life. He was fifty-five, had never married, and didn't seem to be working. "Where does he get his money?" and "What does he do for a living?" were unanswerable questions. From what

I was able to gather from his texts and occasional emails, he was traveling around the world going to Burning Man events with baby-faced tech billionaires.

Do you want to go to Burning Man Africa? he'd text.

No thanks! I'd text back. *Gotta work. On deadline. But you have fun!*

I always got a bit squirrelly when my friends asked about the actual circumstances of how a person like Max happened to have a kid, especially as he hadn't had the kid "on purpose."

Max was one of those people who'd never led a conventional life and was always up front about it. He'd tell his partners that he didn't believe in marriage, nor did he want children. Max knew his personality and lifestyle weren't suited to the raising of small, vulnerable humans.

But Max became a parent anyway. He met an Icelandic woman at a party in Italy and they had sex for the next five days. She called two months later to say four things: she was pregnant, she was going to have the child, she was going to take care of it, and he didn't have to be involved.

Six years passed. Six years in which the son grew up in the small Nordic country, speaking only Icelandic. Occasionally Max would mention his son. "You saw him?" I'd ask, mildly surprised. "How is he?"

"He seems fine. But we can't communicate. He doesn't speak English."

The boy had a simple life. He had a half sister whose father was the opposite of Max—a local fisherman. The boy spent a lot of time outdoors. It was possible that he, too, would have ended up becoming a local fisherman.

But one day the woman decided to seek a better life for her and her children. She took all her savings and moved to the Upper West Side of Manhattan. She was able to get a job as a real estate agent working on twenty-five-hundred-dollar-a-month rentals.

She had enough to get by.

But mostly, because she was in New York City, a place where Max spent a few weeks a year, Max began seeing his son more often. And now, at the age of fifty-five and with no previous experience, Max was trying to feel his way into being a father.

I was determined to help him. After all, he was making an effort and surely this should be encouraged. This, I explained to my friends, was why I had offered to help Max realize his dream of the perfect camping trip with his son.

But not everyone was buying it.

"Don't you think it's weird, this strange woman sending her child to stay at your house?" Tilda Tia asked. She pointed out that as a mother she would never have sent her eight-year-old kid to stay with a woman she'd never met.

I'm not a parent so I wouldn't know. But I can imagine there might be some circumstances under which a mother might send her child away. Like in *Heidi*.

"This isn't *Heidi*," Tilda Tia barked. "I mean, you're not even Max's girlfriend."

"Maybe that's why it's okay," Kitty said. "She's not a threat."

"Do you have any idea what you're getting into?" Tilda Tia was a real den mother. When she stayed at Kitty's, she was always going to the supermarket and cooking meals and yelling at Kitty's other houseguests to clean up their rooms.

She was right. I had no idea of what I was getting into. But I had already committed, prepared for the fact that anything might happen and probably would. As I had no children of my own, I figured at the very least the adventure would be research.

Now I picked up my phone and checked the time and the weather. The heat was going to kick up severe thunderstorms, starting in the next hour or so. Meaning it wouldn't be a good time to set up tents. Because . . . electrocution.

I texted Max: *Where are you?*

When the boy and his father finally arrived by Uber at 10:00 p.m., I'd like to say that I was as gay as a Doris Day housewife, but I wasn't. I was annoyed they'd arrived hours later than promised.

But the arrival of houseguests is like giving birth: you're so happy to see them you immediately forget how irritated you were while waiting for them to show up.

In a display of good parenting, the father rushed the boy into the bathroom while I carted some of their stuff from the driveway to the living room.

As I looked around for where to put the boy's bags, I realized Tilda Tia was right. It was sort of awkward. I wasn't his mother and yet he was staying at my house. His father was not my boyfriend, and yet he was staying at my house, too.

On the other hand, they weren't technically staying *in* the house. They were supposed to be camping in the backyard and hanging out in the barn. They would have their space. I would have mine.

The problem was the impending thunderstorms, which made sleeping in a tent not only unpleasant, but dangerous.

But the boy wasn't interested in being inside. He'd been promised a tent. And he wasn't impressed when his father and I pointed out that the upstairs of the barn was big enough to put up a tent. And it even had a small air conditioner!

It would be cooler. And less buggy. And not subject to the perils of rain.

Nope. The boy wasn't having it. He began ordering his father to put up the tent. I offered to help but was shooed away by the boy.

I went back into the house, poured myself a glass of rosé with ice, and congratulated myself on my luck. Obviously the boy had plans and they didn't include me.

Which meant my relationship with the boy would be simple: I'd be a sort of camp counselor/Airbnb landlady.

Day Two

I woke up the next morning to quiet. Max and the kid were sitting on the couch, silently going through the kid's bag.

I made myself a cup of tea and joined them. Max had slept badly in the tent, and finally at 6:00 a.m. he and the boy had gotten up. They'd already walked to the deli and fed themselves, as evidenced by the greasy paper bags and food wrappings on the table.

"Here," Max said, handing me an envelope.

"What's this?" I said.

"It's a note. From Glotis."

"Who?" I asked.

"Glotis. His mother," Max hissed.

Oh. Right. Glotis.

"Dear Candace," she wrote. "Thank you for looking after my son. I know this will be a once-in-a-lifetime experience for him."

Awwww. That is so sweet. See, Tilda Tia, I wanted to point out. The mother is trusting me with her son. I don't know why she is, but maybe she has a motherly instinct that being around me will somehow be good for him.

The father and I went through his clothes. "Why does he only have two pairs of shorts?" I asked. Max shrugged. "I guess Glotis doesn't have much money to buy him clothes."

I may not know much about children, but clothes I did know. And in this case, I knew exactly what to do.

Max would take the boy shopping and I'd go along to help.

Mommy and Me

Luckily, there were loads of kids' shops on Main Street. There were, I also noticed for the first time, loads of kids. And parents. Families. Falling into step, I wondered what it would be like if this really were my life, if Max and I were married and had a child. It was a bit far-fetched but not impossible I thought as we followed a pair of attractive, early-fortysomething parents and their adorable children into the surf shop. If this really were my life, would I be happier and more content?

Assuming that clothes shopping is "women's work," Max immediately sat down on a couch, leaned back against the cushions, and started texting.

I wasn't bothered. Max's input would only make the situation more confusing and besides, I knew way more about fashion than he did.

"Hey, kid. Look at this," I said, pulling out a yellow T-shirt as I tried to lure the boy toward a circular rack of colorful clothing.

He just stood there, staring at me. Looking lost.

"Okay," I said brightly. "How about . . . sneakers?"

Again, that look. As if he had no idea what I was talking about or why I was with him. A look that said: "You are not my mommy."

Too true. I'm not even Mommy adjacent. I had no authority over the boy and we both knew it.

Luckily, the saleslady came to the rescue. "What a cute little boy," she exclaimed. "What are his sizes?"

For a moment, I was flattered she thought I was young enough to be the boy's mother, but then I remembered that a real mother would know her son's sizes. If I admit that I don't know them, she's going to think I'm one of those bad mommies who doesn't know anything about her own kid.

I was going to have to drop the ruse. I pulled her aside. "Actually, I'm not his mother. In fact, I've only met him once before. And his father only sees him once a year. And he doesn't really speak English."

She got it, of course. Thank god, because shopping, as I would later discover, is one of the many, many things that children cannot do on their own.

The Mother Hens

Of course, I never for one moment thought I could handle the boy and his father by myself. After all, even people who actually have kids have help, right? And sometimes, when they travel with them, these people with the kids bring their own nannies.

Someone at a rich-person party pointed this out to me. I pointed out back that while it was a wonderful concept, Max and I couldn't afford a nanny. And even if we could, there wasn't anyplace to put her. We couldn't ask a nanny to sleep in a pup tent.

Luckily, for help I had all my friends. Like Tilda Tia, they, too, were convinced that the visit was going to be a disaster and I was going to need saving.

I've been known for not being "motherly" ever since I was a kid. When I was a little girl and someone's mother in the neighborhood had a baby, all the little girls would have to troop over with their mothers to see the newborn. The mother would pick it up and hold it out and pass it to one of the little girls and everyone would coo and they'd keep passing the baby around until they got to me and I'd refuse to take it. Besides the fact that I found holding someone else's baby terrifying—what if I dropped it?—it felt like an indoctrination.

In those days, when girls were good at holding babies, they ended up always holding babies. If you were "good with babies" they'd want you to become a babysitter.

I don't think so.

Which was why all my friends had volunteered to help me play Mommy. Queenie and Kitty, both of whom had pools, had offered their houses for the afternoons and even to babysit. Sassy promised to do "sports" with the boy, like badminton and bridge.

Bad Mommy

It's one thing to be a bad mommy theoretically, but it's another to be a bad mommy in real life. Even if you are not technically the mommy.

Indeed, it seems that most women, whether they be biological mothers or not, know what to do in case there is an unmothered child in the vicinity.

Like when a kid arrives at someone's house, you immediately give the kid something to drink. You take him to the bathroom. Give him a cookie. Treat him like a movie executive on a Hollywood set.

Which is exactly what happened when we arrived at Queenie's for a swim. Queenie was what's known as a Yummy Mummy and the boy was immediately taken by her. While she showed the boy to the bathroom, I got a tongue-lashing from my friends.

"Why didn't you say he was so cute!" Sassy said.

"How can you not remember his name? He's a *person*," Kitty scolded.

"Hey. I don't want to push it. I want to respect his boundaries. If he remembers my name, I'll remember his name." I tried to tell them my camp counselor theory but no one bought it.

"Even camp counselors remember the campers' names. It's part of the job, love," Marilyn said, as if I was a dotty old bird.

Seconds later, Queenie came waltzing out to the deck holding the boy's hand. Queenie looked glamorous and chic and put together, and now so, too, did the boy.

He looked happy. And relaxed. And for the first time all day, I relaxed.

But not for long. The other thing about kids is that you can't just entertain them for a few minutes and then they go off and do something on their own.

Nor can you entertain them for a few minutes and then go off and do something on *your* own. It doesn't work like that. It's not a cocktail party.

You have to *keep* entertaining them.

Queenie knew this, being a mother herself. She asked the boy if he could swim and then swam with him in the pool.

Everyone took pictures of Queenie and the boy. Queenie told the boy how handsome he was and what a good boy he was, and we all agreed that Queenie was the best mommy out of all of us. She had the magic touch.

But then, Queenie got called inside by her actual daughter, and Marilyn took over.

Marilyn had grown up on the ocean in Australia and she got the boy to come out of his shell, getting him to talk in his halting English about how he'd lived near the sea in Iceland and it really was dark for two months in the winter and bitterly cold. But then Marilyn, who was sitting out in the broiling sun so the boy could be in the shade under the umbrella, got too hot and had to jump in the pool. Then he cuddled with Kitty, who was also a mom, having been a single mother when she was in her twenties, while Sassy told him stories.

And where was Max during all this mothering? He was in Queenie's air-conditioned house, snoozing on the sofa.

And then the boy got bored. Sassy gave me a look that told me it was my turn to step in and amuse him.

"Hey kid," I said, drawing him away from the group.

"Yazzz?" he asked. He had a big, unsuspecting smile on his face.

"Do you want to learn how to dive?"

"Like how?"

"Like this." I executed a dive from my old swim team days when I, too, had been an eight-year-old.

It worked. Finally the kid wanted to do something with me.

I'll say this about him: He was a fast learner. He had that dive down in about forty minutes. He had tenacity. He didn't give up. And he didn't complain.

Maybe I was going to succeed at this mothering/camp counselor thing after all.

Day Three

Determined to get our mobility worked out, I decided it was time to get the boy on a bike.

I was hoping to get this task done first thing in the morning, which would give me time to work. My plan was to go directly to the bike shop, drop off Max and the boy, and then come home.

But once we got in the car, there was a whole list of other things Max and the boy needed. I groaned. What should have been a thirty-minute excursion was now going to be at least an hour.

There was the twenty-minute stop in the hardware store where we argued about fishing rods and left empty-handed. In the supermarket, we bought all kinds of things I would never eat, like marshmallows, diced fruit, and potato chips. I was beginning to get irritated, thinking about all that extra food in my small kitchen.

Finally we got to the bike store. The boy seemed reluctant to go inside, but I reminded myself that it wasn't my problem. I wasn't the parent.

I reached behind the seat and grabbed a bag of potato chips. For a couple of minutes I just sat there eating chips and enjoying this moment of me time.

"Hello?" Max came marching out of the bike shop.

"Yes?" I leaned out the car window.

"We have a problem." He paused. "You need to come inside."

The atmosphere in the shop wasn't right. The boy was standing in the corner, shoulders slumped as if he wanted to disappear.

Poor kid. It turned out he didn't know how to ride a bike after all. And he didn't want to tell his father because he didn't want to disappoint him.

It was all heartbreakingly sad, but it also meant I'd have to drive Max and the boy everywhere and that wasn't part of the plan. I needed to fix this.

"Maybe he can learn to ride a bike," I suggested.

I pointed out what a terrific opportunity it was, given the fact that my house was ideally located to learn this life-altering skill. There was a park across the street and a cul-de-sac behind my house. The nearby firehouse had a huge parking lot with enough space for practicing turns. I'd practiced there myself at the beginning of the summer.

"Deddy?" the boy said, star struck by the idea. "Will you teach me to ride a bike?"

"Of course I will, son," Max replied.

Success.

Or not. Apparently nothing is simple when you're a parent trying to do things for your kid. The bike shop didn't sell bikes with training wheels, so we had to order it online. This ate up more time and I was beginning to get anxious about neglecting the other parts of my life. The parts that didn't include Max and the boy. I told Max that I absolutely had to get some work done tomorrow morning and that he had to figure out something to do so I could have three hours alone.

"Fine," Max said, rolling his eyes.

"Please Max. I'm not being rude. I love having you guys. It's just that I've got to work."

"You always have to work," he said accusingly, as if this might be the reason we'd broken up fifteen years ago.

I tried to hold my tongue. The thought of writing gave me a sickening helpless feeling, similar to how one feels when a pet is ill. I was on a deadline for a book that wasn't working, which meant I had to somehow work even harder.

And I needed the money.

I didn't want to tell Max, but the house wasn't renovated because I couldn't afford it. At the rate things were going, I might never be able to afford it.

And I certainly wasn't going to tell Max that I had visions of myself in this same unrenovated house thirty years from now alone and wearing these same old clothes—and that was the good version.

Nevertheless, I still felt guilty.

Day Six

The bike with the training wheels arrived!

The people at the bike shop magically put the bike together, and within about three minutes, with no help from his father, the boy was pedaling around the parking lot.

And the smile on his face. I could say it stretched from ear to ear, but it was more than that. It was the smile that makes it all worth it. All the mess, the fuss, the inconvenience of having to feed, clothe, entertain, shepherd, and most of all think obsessively about a small person. When you see the look of joy on a kid's face that tells you that *they get it*—there's nothing like it.

You know you've lived.

And then, like a real parent, I ran back to the car, grabbed my cell phone, and began recording the momentous event.

Day Seven

They say that having children makes you a better person, and, just as I'd hoped, this was happening to Max.

Seeing that his son was a fast learner, Max became determined that the boy would master a number of skills. He would learn how to fish, play tennis, make new friends, and improve his reading level by a grade.

And to prove it, Max and the boy went into the Village on their bikes. They returned with all the Roald Dahl books and also scissors and some construction paper for a diorama. And then—bless them—they took everything out to the barn.

A half hour passed and suddenly the house felt empty. Curious, I went out to see what they were doing and to perhaps offer suggestions.

They shooed me away.

They didn't need me.

And this, I realized, is one of the realities of not having kids. No one needs you. Sure, your dog and your friends need you, but it's not quite the same.

And taking it one step further, when you die, who is going to be bummed out about it? Yes, your friends will be sad but not for that long. And while friends are usually happy to go to your funeral, they don't necessarily want to have to plan it. And finally, who are you going to leave your IRA to?

Assuming you're lucky enough to have an IRA.

That night, as I got ready for bed, I thought about Max and how he suddenly had a purpose in life: his son.

As I closed my eyes, I wondered if I'd missed out.

So the next morning, when Max started talking about his plans and how much fun they were having and how great it would be if he and his son could stay an extra few days, I readily agreed.

Day Ten

"Hey buddy, move it," I snarled under my breath at the slow moving vehicle ahead of me. Why oh why was I in the car again?

I was in the car because it was good for the kid. He was going to sports camp on the grounds of the local private school, and since it was too far to bike, I was driving him. And Max.

The boy was no trouble. Max was another story. He wouldn't stop talking about this stupid Burner wedding he was going to in California and how he needed to dress up like a polar bear but still hadn't ordered the costume from Amazon.

I took a deep breath and looked over to where the summer school kids were starting their day. Sometimes they released balloons; sometimes they wore masks. Today they were playing musical instruments. The banners that hung from the tall glass windows inside the school were a happy purple, green, and orange.

The kids and the few adults were cheerful, clapping their hands.

"Why are they always so happy?" I asked.

"Huh?" Max said.

"Yeah," the kid said. "Deddy, why are they so happy?"

In contrast to those parents and their charges, Max and I were wrecks. Max had taken to wearing barefoot running shoes and the same T-shirt he slept in. I was no better in food-stained shorts and a baggy overwashed fishing shirt.

It was just easier this way.

Gone were the pleasures of the unmarried, middle-aged housewife: The peaceful moments contemplating the greens at the farm stand. Strolling with the dogs at Havens Beach and finding the perfect, shiny orange toenail shell. Getting stoned and dancing to pop music. In short, doing all the mindful, healthy—conscious things middle-aged people are supposed to do to live for another thirty years. The assumption being that one actually has the time to dedicate to raising oneself, as opposed to raising actual children.

Now I woke up with a list as long as my arm of things that needed to be done, bought, fixed, or cleaned up.

But my biggest concern was the boy.

Despite the fact that the boy and I were not close and hardly spoke and I'm pretty sure the kid didn't even like me very much, I had to keep him *safe*. But most of all, I had to make sure he was *happy*.

Somehow, I had developed what I call mommy brain.

For instance, two days ago, when we were picking up the boy from the dock where he'd spent another morning at fishing camp, I suddenly found myself studying the other children. Did they like him? Were they interacting with him? Or was he all alone?

Oh my god. Did he have any friends?

The boy, I noticed, seemed different from the other kids. It wasn't just that he was skinnier. He had a different sensibility that made him appear less civilized. Maybe this was just due to the fact that his father was washing his clothes. They had those deep wrinkles that come from sitting overnight in the dryer.

But so what I thought, as I once again assessed the other children. At least the boy was smart.

And a fast learner. He'd learned how to ride a bike, play tennis, paddleboard, dive, and fish. If we were a family living in the wild, having the boy would come in handy. Not a day goes by when that kid doesn't come home from fishing camp with at least two fish to feed his "parents."

Please tell me how many kids can do that?

Day Twelve

Several packages arrived. Max cut them open and began removing the peanut packing materials, placing them in a large, heavy salad bowl. It wasn't what I would have used, but I did not point this out. Instead, I remembered how

183

considerate the father was being and he was teaching his son. I reminded myself that I was having a happy family experience by osmosis and that hopefully my life would not fall apart because I didn't meet my deadline and I was getting closer and closer to penury.

I leaned in as Max pulled out one of his purchases and unwrapped it. He held it up. "Look son," he said. "A bonsai tree."

"What's a bonsai tree?" the boy asked.

"The bonsai is like a dwarf tree. You know how there are dwarf people? The bonsai is like the same thing but a tree," the father said. Not the words I would have chosen but I've learned not to criticize Max in front of the boy. If I say anything remotely critical about Max, the boy gets upset.

Yesterday, when I was washing a dirty roasting pan and Max was dousing cut-up plums and peaches with alcohol, I made the mistake of calling him weird. The boy immediately became defensive and motioned for me to step outside.

"What's up, kid?" I asked.

"Don't you say anything wrong about my deddy. My deddy is not weird."

"Is weird a bad thing? I think weird is a good thing," I replied.

The boy looked at me suspiciously. "How would you describe my deddy?"

I immediately suspected this was a trick question. "Well, he travels a lot, so I guess he's like James Bond."

No response. Then: "Is Deddy a nerd?"

"I guess you could say he's a bit of a nerd."

"Is being a nerd a good thing or a bad thing?" he asked.

"It's a good thing," I tried to reassure him.

"Then why didn't you say my deddy was a nerd instead of weird?" he demanded.

The kid had got me.

While Max and the boy went through the boxes, I picked up a colored pencil and a pad of paper and began drawing pictures of my poodles. The boy, bored, came over to see what I was doing. Then he started drawing a camel.

The house was quiet save for the sound of our pencils on paper.

This was nice I realized. It was nice to sit quietly in the living room drawing.

If I had a kid, would I try to improve my drawing skills again, I wondered. I crumpled up the poodles and attempted a horse head instead.

As I drew, I wondered what it would be like if me, Max, and the boy spent more time like this together. And what did the boy's mother really think about the situation? After all, I was Max's ex-girlfriend. Did she worry that Max and I might get back together and then we'd raise the child instead?

"Is she pretty?" I'd asked Max.

"Who?"

"His mother."

Max shrugged. "She's pretty in that Icelandic way. They're all pretty."

I got her last name out of him and found a few images of her online. She was, of course, stunningly beautiful.

I picked up a new piece of paper and attempted a sketch of the kid's profile.

He leaned over to see what I was drawing. "Is that supposed to be me?" he said, affronted. "You made the nose too big."

"Yes, that's true," I admitted. "I didn't get the proportions exactly right, okay?"

The kid sighed. I sighed. I went back into my office and the kid went back to his father, probably to complain about me.

Day Fourteen

A huge thunderstorm from the night before left the campground soaked. It also flooded the barn, which meant I had to manually sweep out the water with an array of brooms.

It was one of those unavoidable tasks that for some reason only I could do.

The males would have to deal with their tents.

Having completed my task, I headed back to the house.

Surprise! Max made us delicious BLT sandwiches, including a couple of extra sandwiches for later. He really was turning out to be a great dad. While we ate, we talked about the storm the night before. Max tried to explain to his son how electricity worked.

I smiled. Max offered to clean up the kitchen so I could write.

I had peace for ten minutes.

"Come quick!" Max shouted.

"What?" I gasped and, in a panic, hurried out of the house after him. "What is it?"

Max peeled back the flap on the tent.

I peeked inside. The tent wasn't waterproof and was now strewn with wet clothes. Meaning a morning's worth of laundry.

"Okay guys!" I said, trying to inspire them in my determined-to-be-cheerful coaching voice. "Why don't you take out all your clothes and carry them to the porch and then I can get started washing them."

Max glared. He informed me that he was going to use this as a teachable moment about lightning and wet tent safety and I should go away.

Thirty minutes later, I went back out to check on them. They'd done nothing. I didn't know what they had been doing, but it wasn't taking their wet clothes to the porch.

"Hey," I said. "Can you guys get to it?"

Max suddenly had a hissy fit. "I wasn't aware that you were running this place like a factory. I was in the middle of *discussing something with my son.*"

"And that would be fine," I retorted. "If I didn't potentially have four loads of laundry ahead of me."

I stormed back to my office, furious.

Kids and men have many common traits. Such as: Starting a project and not finishing it. Leaving messes for other people to clean up. Not understanding "messes" or what constitutes one.

And all of this is probably okay, unless you are playing the caretaking role in the relationship. Which means you are mothering, you are cleaning up, you are silent, you are putting others first along with their needs, even if—and especially if—their "needs" require that you spend less time on your needs.

In other words, you have volunteered to make yourself a second-class citizen. Meaning: A person whom no one ever thanks. Who does the really hard stuff. And who is little appreciated. Women, as far as I'm concerned, should take away Mother's Day from the male-run hearts-and-flowers companies that make millions on our sympathies and put it back in the hands of the actual mothers. Who could use some actual help.

Five minutes later, after mentally cursing Max, he brought in a pile of wet laundry and helped me load it into the washer.

I reminded myself to take a deep breath. Everything was going to be fine.

On my way back to work, I saw that Max had left the extra sandwich on the table. I stole a little piece of bacon and thought that perhaps this would be a good day after all.

I had peace for three minutes.

"Oh no," Max shouted.

"What?" I said, rushing out.

"Your dog ate my sandwich!"

Day Fifteen

Was it really the end of the month? How had so much time passed? And so much emotion?

At 2:00 p.m. on a sunny Sunday afternoon, Max and I were perched gingerly on the edge of a high bleacher, waiting for the boy to get an award from the sports camp. I could tell the other parents were old hands at this, this game watching. They sat in the middle of the bleachers in a huddle, and they knew not just their own kid's name but the names of the other kids as well. If I'd had kids, I suppose this would have been my life, too—sitting around green spaces wearing baseball caps and being part of a family. The parents all seemed very nice—there's something about kids that makes most adults behave—but they were also at least a decade younger than Max and me, with faces that still had that hopeful glow that all this was going to make sense someday.

Me and Max, we stood out.

We didn't know where to sit. Or what to do.

Not being an actual parent, I assumed the real parents didn't have this problem. I envied the fact that their lives had a pattern. Predictable, perhaps, but also comforting. Because when you have kids, you know what you're supposed to do with your life. You know what's supposed to happen and when.

If you're childless and single, you don't have the pattern. You don't know how it's supposed to go down. And so, while I was waiting for the coach to call the boy's name, I was a nervous wreck.

What if he calls the boy's name last? What if he forgets and doesn't call his name at all? And what if he runs out of trophies before he gets to the boy? My heart would break.

I think I need to have words with that coach. I think I need to give him a little pop on the snout.

"Hey!" I shouted.

"Hey," Max nudged me. "Aren't you going to take a video?"

Day Seventeen

The boy and his father left on a Tuesday in a beat-up gray van driven by a local taxi guy. It crossed my mind that the van might not make it to NYC, but as usual I was the only person worried about this.

In any case, there was no choice. They needed space for the bike and the tents, and the finished diorama, which Max and the boy cleverly nestled into a cardboard box.

They loaded the van and shut the doors. From the stoop, I watched as the van backed cautiously down the driveway. I waved, but I didn't linger.

I went straight to my computer where I watched the video I made for the boy.

The video was a revelation. The vacation appeared to be everything Max and I had hoped for. The backyard looked like a real campsite, with two tents and two charcoal grills and a badminton net. There was the boy learning to paddle-board on the bay in front of Kitty's house with one of the poodles. And there he was in the harbor, having just gotten off the fishing boat, displaying the two large fish he caught. And finally, he's walking along the side of the playing field to take his trophy from soccer camp.

And through the whole thing you could see the kid was *happy*. He was laughing, joking. He was having fun.

And there was Max. Dear old Max. He was having a great time, too, standing with his hands proudly on his hips as the boy rode the bike all the way down the street for the first time without training wheels.

I wondered if the kid would remember me. Probably not. But if he does, I'll be that weird lady whose house he stayed in during that summer when he learned to ride a bike.

Who doesn't need that person in their life?

I titled the file with the boy's name—Dagmar—and hit Save.

CHAPTER EIGHT

THE BOYFRIEND EXPERIENCE

MARILYN AND I have boyfriends!

It's kind of a miracle. Up until we got our MNBs (my new boyfriends) we considered ourselves diehard single girls. We couldn't imagine being with a man and praised ourselves for not needing one. Sure, sometimes we'd get a little bummed out—are we really going to go to bed alone for the rest of our lives—but then, like good, sensible women, we'd remind ourselves of how lucky we were to have a bed.

And not just a bed but a room of our own in a house of our own.

Since we weren't counting on a man to come into our future, we weren't looking. We'd said no to fix ups and didn't go to bars or restaurants where we could meet men. Mostly we hung out at Kitty's, entertaining ourselves with stories of how we would renovate our houses if we ever got the money.

Meaning, we had lowered our chances of meeting someone to just about zero.

And that was okay. I'd done a bit of research on the kinds of men who were available, and they didn't look promising. Especially when it came to age-appropriate men. The problem seemed to be that unlike the cubs, middle-aged men were often still of the mindset that women over fifty weren't all that appealing. Especially when it was so easy for them to find not just younger women, but women who were eager to begin the reproductive lifestyle all over again with them.

The Hot-Drop

Take, for instance, the "hot-drop." Unlike men who initiate the divorce and often have another relationship teed up, the hot-drop guy finds himself unintentionally single. It could be that his wife has died. Or his wife may have cheated or fallen in love with someone else. She may have simply become bored with him and couldn't picture spending another day much less another thirty years listening to the same jokes. In any case, he's single or about to become single, and he won't be for long.

You see, there is really nothing wrong with the hot-drop. Indeed, it's the opposite: there is, perhaps, too much right with him. This is what Kitty discovered when she ran into Harold at an art opening.

She hadn't seen him for years but recognized him immediately. He had a cool downtown haircut, now sprinkled with gray, but his face had hardly aged. And he still had a big job in the art world. When he mentioned that he was divorced as well—or about to be—Kitty couldn't believe her luck. She'd had a little crush on him years ago when they used to be part of the same circle, but had lost touch. And now here they were again.

This time displaying photographs of their children to each other on their phones. Kitty's daughter was over thirty and married, but Harold's daughter was a real child, an adorable ten-year-old girl named Agnes. Kitty suddenly felt maternal. She realized she wouldn't mind remothering such a gorgeous child who was clearly full of personality.

As they left the opening to go have a drink somewhere else, Kitty wondered if her luck was about to change.

Harold certainly seemed interested. At the bar, he kept touching her hand with his fingers when he wanted to make a point and when they kissed goodnight, he gave her an actual kiss on the lips.

That night, as Kitty lay in bed, she had a fantasy that she and Harold would fall in love and get married and that somehow, by doing so, she would be able to leapfrog all of the issues of MAM. Why shouldn't she be the lucky one? The one who gets through this middle-aged dating thing unscathed by sliding into an even better relationship?

Kitty never heard from Harold, although she texted him three times and called him twice. Six months later, she ran into him again at another art opening. But this time he was with a woman. She, too, had a cool downtown haircut. But she looked young. She didn't have a line on her face. Kitty decided she couldn't be more than twenty-five.

And so, when she looked from Harold to the young woman, the words just slipped out of her mouth. "And how do you two know each other?" she asked. "Are you related?" Perhaps, she suggested, Harold was the young woman's uncle.

The young woman gave her a look of disgust. "We're engaged," she said.

When she walked away, Harold reassured Kitty that it was okay. Although his fiancée looked like a teenager she was actually almost forty. And then he gave Kitty a beaming smile and informed her that he was about to become a father again.

And this is the problem with the hot-drop. No matter how age appropriate he is and no matter how great you are, in less time than it takes to get a blow-dry he has not just a new relationship but a whole new family.

The He's as Old as Your Father Guy

The reality of the hot-drop odds can cause some women to try to game the odds in their favor by "playing" the game, i.e., dating a man who is fifteen, twenty, even twenty-five years older. Which means, given the fact that you are now middle-aged yourself, a man who is seventy? Seventy-five? Eighty?

You wouldn't think there would be a large contingent of men around that age who are "dating." But when you think about demographics and how so many of the boomers are now in their later years, it makes sense that there's a crop of sixty-, seventy-, and even eightysomething men out there acting like they are thirty-five.

I encountered one of these men at a party given by a married couple in their early sixties. There were lots of fifty-something single women and two or three of these senior-age players, or SAPs. These are older single men of means, meaning they have enough money to add it to their list of attributes and are often still employed in a lesser version of the high-powered career they once had. At some point during the party I must have talked to one of these men, because a few days later, Ron, the host of the party, contacted me to let me know that a fellow named Arnold was interested in taking me out.

Ron was very excited about this. And impressed. He said Arnold was a big deal and he really admired the guy. He'd played Ivy League football and he was once an oilman and a newspaper magnate and all the Park Avenue hostesses were always inviting him to their parties. He was sought after.

I thought I remembered the guy: a tall, thick battle-ax type who was definitely older—too old for me I'd decided.

"How old is he?" I asked.

"He's a little bit older than I am," Ron said. "Sixty-eight?"

These guys often lie about their ages. They fudge, somehow forgetting about that truth-telling device called the internet. Sure enough, when I googled him, Arnold turned out to be seventy-five.

That made him much closer to my father's age than mine. My father was eighty-three; Arnold was just eight years younger. They couldn't have been more different though. My father is very conservative. Arnold apparently is not. According to Ron, Arnold used to be somewhat of a notorious wild man who went to Studio 54. Even to this day, Arnold still has much younger girlfriends, the last one being forty-five.

"I don't know how he does it," Ron said.

I wanted to tell Ron that I didn't want to be the one to find out.

And so I tried to say no. Peer pressure, however, is one of the things I hadn't counted on in middle age. And when it came to dating, it turns out there was a lot of it.

My friends kept reminding me that it was good to go out and it was really good that someone had actually asked me out. When was the last time that had happened? Of course I should go. What was the harm in it? And besides, you never know.

Of course, the problem with "you never know" is that so often you actually do know.

I knew—or I was convinced I knew—that I was not going to date a seventy-five-year-old man no matter how wonderful he was. What if he fell down? I didn't spend my life working this hard to end up taking care of a strange old person.

But every time I tried to explain this, I realized how ageist and judgy and anti–love hopeful I sounded.

Because I didn't know, did I? I didn't know what was going to happen. What if I fell in love with him? In which case, his age wouldn't matter, right? Plus, I didn't want to be *that* woman—you know, that shallow creature who cares more about practicality than the blind illusions of love.

Plus, as Ron reminded me, I must feel so honored that a man "as powerful as Arnold" wanted to spend time with me.

In preparation for the date, I went to Sassy's house and we looked at photographs of Arnold on the internet. His photos went back about thirty years. He'd been a big man and rather handsome.

"Oh honey," Sassy said. "He could turn out to be absolutely wonderful. You must keep an open mind."

And so arrangements for a date were negotiated. We could have gone to a restaurant in my town, but Arnold really wanted me to see his house, which was in another town about fifteen minutes away. He could pick me up and take me to his town and then I could always spend the night at his house if I needed to and he could drive me back to my house in the morning.

A sleepover? With a seventy-five-year-old man I didn't know?

I don't think so.

I was finally able to negotiate that I would drive my car to his house and we would walk to the restaurant and then back to his house. And then I would drive home.

Or spend the night he suggested again, in a friendly manner.

Sassy scolded me over these arrangements. "Why didn't you demand that he pick you up?"

"Because he doesn't drive at night. Which means if he picks me up, I'm trapped. I'm on his schedule. At least if I have my car I can get away if I have to."

As it was, I was making him start the date much earlier than he would have liked, at 6:00 p.m. He wanted to start it at 8:00, which meant the date might go on until 11:00. I didn't want to be with Arnold at an hour that could be construed as "bedtime."

When I pulled into Arnold's driveway, he was waiting for me outside. I thought that was sweet of him, but mostly he wanted to show me where to park my car so it wouldn't get towed and the neighbors wouldn't complain.

We went inside the house. Arnold shut the door and locked it.

I hoped Arnold would not turn out to be a psycho killer.

This reminded me of what Emma had said about the men online: "Just don't be a psycho killer." It was extraordinary how this sentiment still crossed all demographics, dating methods, and ages.

If Arnold were a seventy-five-year-old killer though, he'd have to be pretty stupid to murder *me*. Everyone knew about our date and he'd be the first suspect.

I took a deep breath and reminded myself to be nice.

I wasn't feeling nice. I was feeling uncomfortable and a little bit loaded for bear. I was angry for allowing myself to be put in this situation even though it was only for three hours and it was one meal and what was wrong with me?

I reminded myself of what Ron had said, of what society would say to women like me: I should be grateful to have a date with a man like Arnold.

And so I did the usual: I admired his contemporary art, which he'd bought years ago when he owned a gallery and had hung out with artists. I oohed and ahhed over his rare book collection. When he offered to take me on a tour of the house, I agreed. The rooms were masculinized modern spaces with lots of windows, metal, and glass. There was no clutter. Everything was in its place, a place, I sensed, that had been its place for a very long time.

Despite the airy spaces, the house wasn't particularly large. Within seconds of the tour, we were in his bedroom.

A wall of windows framed an expansive vista of lawn and gardens. I admired the view.

The scenery, however, was not the best part of the bedroom.

Did I want to know what the best part of the bedroom was Arnold asked.

"Sure," I said gamely.

He grinned. "The bed. I've had it for twenty years," he said proudly. "This bed has brought me good luck. I've had a lot of great sex on that bed." He paused and looked at me meaningfully. "And I hope to have a lot more in the future."

I took a better look at the bed. The sheets were slightly rumpled, and I couldn't help but wonder if Arnold had been having some kind of "go" at it before I'd arrived. I pictured him naked on the sheets, his great white belly sluicing from side to side.

"Well, bully for you," I said. I suggested that I needed a drink.

An open bottle of red wine and two glasses sat on the counter in the kitchen. It had that sort of dusty, neglected air that kitchens get when no one uses them.

I apologized and said I didn't drink red wine. Only white or rosé.

"But Ron told me you drink red wine. I asked him and he said you drank red and so I went out and got us a nice bottle."

I wanted to point out that Ron didn't know a thing about me and so it was illogical to ask Ron what kind of wine I preferred. I didn't say it, of course. Instead, I attempted to negotiate.

"I'd prefer white if you have it."

"Are you sure you don't want the red? It's a really good bottle. And don't worry about drinking. You can always spend the night here."

"Hahahaha." My sarcastic laugh hid a head rush of hot annoyance. I thought about making some excuse and leaving, but I couldn't think of one that would warrant such a response without making me look crazy and causing a furor among the social set who had condoned this pairing.

In other words, I wasn't yet ready to be socially ostracized in order to get away from Arnold.

He showed me his pool next. It was small and kidney shaped. "Do you want to go swimming?" he asked.

"No thanks."

"Why not?"

"I don't have my bathing suit."

"You can swim naked," he said.

"I don't think so."

"Well, you're welcome to come here anytime you want and swim," he said, with what seemed to be a generous smile that was yet completely oblivious to my raging discomfort.

"Arnold." I sighed. "I'm never going to come here and swim in your pool."

"Why not?" he asked.

"It's too small. I like to swim laps. I'm sorry but your pool is basically a bath tub."

Arnold laughed suggestively. The good thing about men like Arnold is that you can say pretty much anything you want to them and they won't be insulted. They're so arrogant and sure of themselves it never crosses their mind that a woman *could* be insulting them.

* * *

We strolled, slowly, to the restaurant.

"You look young and spry," Arnold said. "You must exercise. How old are you?"

"I'm nearly sixty."

Arnold looked taken aback.

Apparently Ron had lied not just about Arnold's age to me but also about my age to Arnold. The difference was, I knew enough to google, and Arnold did not.

"Well that's terrific," he said. "So we're in the same place. We're both looking for companionship."

Of all the micro- and macroaggressions of aging, the worst one is when you discover you've crossed the bridge from wanting a *relationship*, with all that entails, to having to settle for its lesser cousin: *companionship.*

A relationship implies a dynamic partnership where people are going to get something done. Companionship implies the opposite: people are going to keep each other company while they mostly just sit there.

Of course, men like Arnold don't have to settle for anything.

After years of having hot young girlfriends—he could still get girls as young as twenty-five if he wanted he explained— he had an epiphany. He was with a woman who was thirty-five and it was all going great when it hit him: he didn't have anything to say to her. It turned out this wasn't a fluke. He no longer had anything to say to any woman who was under thirty-five. They were just too young. And so, reluctantly, he'd had to rethink his requirements and decided to up his age group. He would now consider dating women who were thirty-five to possibly fifty.

I took a good, long look at Arnold. Some men do look younger than their years, and there are plenty of attractive seventy-five-year-old guys, but Arnold was not one of them. His glory days on the Ivy League football fields were long gone. It was impossible to imagine him as any kind of a sexual draw. On the other hand, society colludes to tell men they're a little bit better than they actually are while it tells women they're a little bit worse.

I, however, was not society.

"Listen Arnold," I said. "You cannot believe that these twenty-five- and thirty-five- and even forty-five-year-old women with whom you are supposedly having sex are actually attracted to you."

Arnold considered this, and then, strangely, he agreed. Even if the women weren't per se attracted to him, he explained, the system still worked in his favor. And the reason for it was that women were greedy.

Arnold explained it like this: The world was filled with women with okay jobs like real estate broker or hair stylist or yoga instructor and a lot of them had kids and ex-husbands who didn't pay child support or were alcoholics—the whole panoply of human suffering—and while these women had enough to get by, they wanted a much bigger lifestyle. They wanted *the* lifestyle. A lifestyle they couldn't afford.

They wanted expensive handbags!

And that's where Arnold and his ilk came in.

You'd think that after all his accomplishments in the world, Arnold would have had some broader empathy for these women in difficult situations but nope. When Arnold thought about women, when he described women, about as much depth as he could grant them was as handbag hoarders who used sex to fuel their addiction.

Did he care that he, too, was being "used"?

Absolutely not.

Men, Arnold explained, don't care why a woman is having sex with them as long as she *is* having sex with them.

Plus, he reminded me, men have the power because if one woman doesn't meet their demands, there's always another woman who will. It's a script that men with money control and continue to control even into old age—as long as they're able to provide something some "greedy" woman wants. Like an expensive handbag.

But what if the world were different and the income stream flowed in the opposite way? Not toward Arnold but to those women with the kids and no way to make more money. What if the world were completely different and there were no women who "needed" to have sex with Arnold for any reason?

What the hell would happen to Arnold?

✳   ✳   ✳

I went over to Sassy's house and told her all about the date. We agreed it was the same old, same old: you think a guy is maybe going to turn out to be great and at least have one or two unexpected depths, but then he turns out to just be another sexist jerk looking to get his wienie waxed. This, Sassy explained, was the reason why she'd never managed to get married. She'd be in a relationship for a while and then all of a sudden, something wild and independent and fierce would rise up inside her and say, *Why?*

"I finally figured out that it's not possible to have a real partner in life because relationships are inherently sexist," she said. "You have to be the mommy and the caretaker and when they want to have sex, you have to want to have sex and at a certain point a part of me would say, 'Why? Why am I doing all this for you and what am I getting out of it?'"

And there it was, the question that women are never supposed to ask when it comes to relationships. What am I getting out of it?

Because who cares, right? Who cares what the woman is getting out of it as long as someone else is getting something out of her.

And then we did what we always do when we come up against the intractable realities of life.

We laughed.

The Spouse-Child

Here is another common type who is now unfettered and on the loose. Like the hot-drop, he has also become divorced unintentionally. But unlike the hot-drop, he is not, well, hot.

Indeed, he's usually pretty much of a mess. Which isn't, perhaps, surprising. This guy is the one women are referring to when they make comments like: "I have three children. Two actual children and my husband."

Like most unions, the spouse-child's marriage began with the best intentions—as a contemporary marriage where both partners worked and would try to share everything equally. But somewhere along the way, usually after the second child, it all falls apart. Even if she works—and she most probably does—the responsibilities of running the house and taking care of the children fall to her. When she asks her husband to help out, he pouts or gets angry or needs so many instructions it's easier to do it herself.

And that's the first brick in the wall of resentment.

This, of course, is no reason to get divorced. If it were, nearly everyone would be. Indeed, the tricky thing about the spouse-child is that outside the house, he's a perfectly nice guy. He does all the things perfectly nice guys do. He goes to work. He goes to his kids' school events. He's there—physically anyway—for holidays and birthdays. He could be anyone's husband.

But at home it's a different story. It's not just that he doesn't do his share of the housework, but it's also that as time goes on he does less and less of his share of everything. He's there but not there. Not intellectually, not emotionally, and not sexually. He doesn't take care of himself, makes no effort, and lets himself go. He gains weight, which makes his sleep apnea worse. At night he disappears into his snoring machine.

Eventually, he stops going through the motions at all.

Meanwhile, his wife lies next to him in despair, staring at the ceiling and wondering what the hell happened to her marriage and how the hell she ended up like this and how the hell is she supposed to fix it?

If her husband does understand how unhappy she is, he ignores it. Because, while he isn't necessarily happy, the spouse-child's marriage is convenient for him. Like the child his wife declares him to be, he makes very little effort but nevertheless gets most of his needs met. And for his needs that aren't met, well, there's always the internet.

And so, while he's there but not there, he isn't planning on going anywhere anytime soon.

This is something his wife instinctually knows. And what she realizes is that if she doesn't do something now, if she doesn't pull the trigger on this marriage, she's only going to get older and unhappier until one day she's too old and tired to leave.

So, while the spouse-child hides out in his "home office"—a misnomer since he's never produced any actual work there—his wife starts thinking about how great it would be if he were gone. How much she could use his closet space and the time spent picking up after him.

How much better it would be if he just went away and never came back.

And one day and seemingly out of the blue, she asks for a divorce.

The spouse-child is taken off guard and throws a tantrum. In his mind, he's blameless. It's all her fault.

Chances are, he will fight bitterly against the divorce. Just as he was noncompliant in the house, so will he be noncompliant with the court.

The divorce will drag on forever. Even the spouse-child's lawyer will say his client is crazy.

Without anyone to take care of him, he falls apart. Kicked out of his house and with no place to live, it isn't unusual for the spouse-child to move back in with his mother and start drinking too much.

In short, he goes through what is basically a male version of MAM.

The good news is that he is not a lost cause. Living with his mother and looking into the disappointed eyes of his now-teenage children every other weekend, he realizes he does not want to be a loser. And so he gets himself together. He goes to the gym. He finds a job and his own place to live, learns to do his own shopping and laundry. Thus rehabilitated, he's ready to get back into the dating pool. And now it is entirely possible that he will end up becoming, yes, one woman's ex-husband but also another woman's new guy.

The My New Boyfriend Phenomenon

It was Fourth of July weekend. Over at Kitty's house we were talking summer goals.

Mine was, as usual, the least admirable: go to parties at rich people's houses and drink free champagne.

And just like magic, there it was: a text from Max.

He'd suddenly decided to fly in from Spain to go to a tech-boy billionaire's birthday party in East Hampton and did I want to go?

The next afternoon as I was getting ready to go out, I found myself taking special care in my appearance. Was this a sign perhaps that I was no longer allergic to the idea of meeting someone? This party might be—unlike Kitty's backyard—an actual place to do that.

Or not.

Max arrived a bit late and as we hurried into my car, he informed me that he was going to take a chemically manufactured designer drug called Special K and go into a K-hole and I should go with him.

No. "I'm not going to take a horse tranquilizer," I said.

"Just a little, babes. It's fantastic. You don't have to sleep for twenty-four hours."

"Don't you realize how horrible that sounds?"

"What's wrong with you?" Max said. "You used to be fun."

When my friends would question why I wouldn't get back together with Max and I said I just couldn't, this was the reason. I couldn't travel around the world going to burnings and closings and billionaires' birthday parties and getting into a K-hole. It just wasn't the kind of life I wanted to lead.

As we made our way down a quarter-mile driveway that led to the billionaire's house, we were stopped three times by three different sets of guards who checked our names on the list and shined a flashlight through the interior of the car to make sure we weren't sneaking in uninvited guests. One even checked the trunk.

"Oh, for god's sake," I barked at him. "We're middle-aged people. Do we look like we'd hide people in our cars?"

The guy shone the flashlight in my face. "You'd be surprised what I've seen middle-aged people do."

The party was in full swing on a large terrace behind the house decorated with holograms and unicorn lights. There was a marble fire pit and two tiki bars and a large patio filled with tables and chairs for dining. Beyond that was a covered tent where a line of caterers prepared dinner. Farther back was an Olympic-size pool with a covered outdoor bar. All ending, finally, in thirty-foot-high hedges.

Max was immediately surrounded by a small group of "burners"—his pals from Burning Man who were dressed like a circus troupe. For some reason, they were younger than

I'd expected. Then I realized this was due to my warped perspective. I hadn't been around thirtysomethings for so long I'd forgotten how young they still looked. And how excited and enthusiastic they were. About everything.

I was definitely going to need a glass of champers to deal with it.

I elbowed through the crowd. More thirtysomethings! But these were the opposite of the burners. These were the super straights. Dressed in button-down shirts and blue blazers, they were Midwest conservatives. Married, with children.

I wondered which direction to go in. To the fire pit, with the people in costumes who were on Special K? Or to the fresh-faced couples full of expectations that it was all going to work out for them?

And suddenly, I'd never felt so out of place in my life. And so very, very—single.

And that's when I spotted him.

That Guy.

That Guy. You remember That Guy. I couldn't remember That Guy's name, but I remembered other things about him. Like how I'd always been curious about That Guy. He was very tall and kind of aloof.

People said he was smart. Kitty had taken me to a party at his house years ago and he'd taken me on a tour and I remembered that he talked to me like I was a real person. But then Kitty said he only dated other really tall, beautiful women from countries like Sweden.

And now here he was standing in the comforting yellow light of the house. He must have recognized me because he was smiling.

Tonight, for some reason, That Guy was awfully happy to see me. I wasn't sure if it was because he was actually happy to see *me* or if it was because he didn't know anyone else either.

No matter. We began chatting enthusiastically. About what we were doing this summer and where we lived. About the dinner party we both happened to be invited to the next night at the home of the F. Scotts'.

This coincidence seemed to delight him. He had someone take a picture of us, which he then sent to the F. Scotts, with the sentiment that we were looking forward to seeing them tomorrow.

He showed me the picture and I groaned. When I'd left my house, I'd been under some kind of mistaken impression that I looked sexy.

I did not. My hair needed a trim. I looked, as Kitty would later say, "boring."

And then, because I knew I was going to see him the next night anyway, I excused myself and went back to the bar, where I looked around and was once again struck by how much I didn't know these people. Like, not even enough to have friends of friends in common.

That Guy materialized at my side. "Can I get you a glass of champagne?" He had a deep, soothing voice, like an old-timey radio announcer.

"Thanks. But you really don't have to."

"I think I do," he said, with the nicest smile.

After that, MNB did not leave my side. He held my drink as I went through the buffet line and made sure I had my cutlery. He found us a table, sitting next to the actual billionaire who owned the house, who was from Chicago and was with his two college-student daughters, who took us on a tour of the house. It had fifteen bedrooms and was appointed like a boutique hotel. There was a large gym, sauna and steam rooms, massage and treatment room, a hair and makeup room, and a home theater that could fit a hundred people. The kitchen had its own pastry and ice-cream chef.

That's the thing about rich people. They can have anything they want but like everyone else, they all just want ice cream.

We went into another room, which was set up like a disco. MNB and I danced. He was a pretty good dancer. Then MNB heard about another party that was close to my house, so we decided to go there. But first I needed to find Max to tell him I was leaving.

We discovered him on his hands and knees in the grass, acting like a dog. "Pet me. Pet me!" he said.

"Max!" I said sharply.

I tried to introduce the two men, but Max wasn't having it. He began howling at the moon.

I gave up.

"Is he okay? Should we do something?" MNB asked.

"He'll be fine. I guess he's in a K-hole. Apparently he gets into K-holes all the time."

"I don't get it," MNB said. "Did you really date that guy?"

"It was . . ." I did the math. "Fifteen, twenty years ago? In any case, he was different back then."

MNB had a car and driver. On the way to the next party, we started making out. MNB was a good kisser and he made me feel like I was a good kisser, too. I hadn't kissed anyone for a while, so this gave me hope.

Later, when he dropped me off at my house, he said the strangest thing. He said, "I really like you. I have instincts about people and I'm not often wrong. I think you and I could be really good together."

"Ha. Get out of here," I said, pushing him out the door. "You don't even know me."

As I got into bed, I wondered if maybe I wasn't out of the relationship game after all.

I woke up to a text from MNB saying he hoped I'd slept well and sending me the info about the car service pickup that evening, which he'd arranged so that I wouldn't have to drive to the F. Scotts' and back. This was slightly embarrassing. I didn't even know him and he was sending a car to pick me up.

I went over to Kitty's. "You won't believe what happened. I made out with this guy."

"Who?" she demanded.

"You know him," I said, by way of explanation. "That Guy."

"That Guy?" Kitty was gobsmacked. Then she started laughing. "You made out with That Guy?"

"What's so funny?"

"You and That Guy. I would never in a million years put you two together."

"Well we saw each other at a party and we made out. And he gave me a ride home. And he's sending me a car to take me to the F. Scotts'."

"That's great," Kitty said. "Then we can go together."

I'd forgotten that Kitty was going to the F. Scotts', too.

"Can't," I said, remembering. "I've got that thing at the library first."

The "thing at the library" was a panel discussion with Erica Jong and Gail Sheehy. It was one of those events they do every month at the Bridgehampton Library. Originally it was called Three Women Writers, but Erica thought that was sexist so now it was called, simply, Three Writers. I hadn't told any of my friends about it because the evening was going to be cold and rainy, the event was held outdoors, and the audience would mostly consist of informed senior citizens. But I'd made the mistake of telling MNB about it and now he was coming.

In fact, he'd constructed a complicated arrangement in which the car would pick me up and take me to Bridge-hampton, then would pick him up in Southampton and take him back to Bridgehampton, where he would meet me at the library. Then we were going to go across the street to meet Marilyn and her sister, and then the car was going to take us to Water Mill for the F. Scotts' dinner.

I couldn't imagine how Kitty was going to fit into this scheme. "We'll give you a ride home, okay?" I said.

The library event was as miserable as I'd predicted. The temperature had dropped, and not one of us was prepared for the weather, so we were sporting various coats and wraps that had been procured for us from the audience.

MNB arrived toward the end. He stood out not just for his height but also for the fact that he was one of the few men there. At that point, the conversation onstage had turned to the inevitable—men and how much they sucked but not all men.

As I was pointing out how maybe it wasn't "all men" but it was certainly "enough men," I saw MNB waylaid by a woman commonly described as a little old lady.

She turned to him and said, "You seem like a very nice, empathetic man. What are you doing here?"

MNB laughed. "I came to see her," he said, indicating me.

Later, at the dinner, like we were already a couple, we told this story to the F. Scotts. "You could both do a lot worse," they said.

And so began a whirlwind boyfriend experience. MNB did everything right. He did everything a woman should want when it comes to romance. He sent flowers. He took me to see *Hello, Dolly!* and walked me back home singing, "Hello, Candace!" He took me on island vacations. We had couple massages and did yoga. He said, "I know you haven't been spoiled in a long time and I want to spoil you."

"But why?" I asked.

"Because you deserve to be spoiled."

In the mornings, I'd look down at the pretty bowl of cut-up fruit he'd prepared for me for breakfast and think, Why me?

"I don't get it," I said to Sassy. "How did I meet this great age-appropriate guy who has his own money and his own house and is really nice . . . and he wants to be my boyfriend?"

She said, "Honey, you've worked hard, you've done the work, and you deserve it."

Perhaps I had, but we all know that just because a woman deserves something good, it doesn't always mean she's going to get it.

Did I deserve to be spoiled by a wonderful single man who didn't appear to have anything glaringly wrong with him? Of course I did.

And so does every other woman. But how often does it happen? Almost never.

Why should the universe have singled me out for this particular carnival ride?

And then Marilyn called. "I think I might have a new boyfriend," she said.

When I'm Sixty-Four

Like me and MNB, they, too, had met at a party in the Hamptons. And like me and MNB, it turned out that they, too, knew lots of people in common but had never met.

Until now. At the party, they talked for three hours. The next day, he called her up and asked if she wanted to go for a walk on the beach. They went at sunset and the sky was pink, and it turned out he lived near the beach and he was a surfer.

He also had an apartment in Brooklyn and a cool tech business that made environmental designs.

And he was sixty-four.

Was that too old? Marilyn wondered.

I pointed out that sixty-four was the current age of her last ex-boyfriend, with whom she'd broken up several years ago. Meaning that even though sixty-four "sounded" old, in reality, it was just the current age of people we used to know when we all were younger.

In any case, it didn't matter. Because the best thing about this guy was that he really listened. And he really cared. And most of all, he, too, was really, really nice.

Nice Guys Finally Finish First?

And so, after all those years of barely dating, Marilyn and I somehow had boyfriends. We couldn't believe it. And neither could our friends.

Gathering at Kitty's to analyze these new developments, we made a list of the MNB attributes:

1. MNBs are nice guys. And they're known in the world as being nice. There isn't a string of bad gossip attached to their names. There are no rumors of them having cheated; there aren't people going around muttering under their breath, "Yeah, but he's an asshole." They don't have a string of ex-wives who hate them.

In fact, "nice" is the hallmark personality trait of the MNB. And while nice didn't matter so much in one's twenties and thirties, now it is about the best quality a person can have. Nice is safety from the storm in a world that, it turns out, is not so very nice after all.

2. They're grown-ups. They have their own lives and their own places to live. Which means they know how to do everyday stuff. Like shopping. And washing the dishes and doing the laundry. And feeding themselves.

3. They're not alcoholics or drug addicts.

4. They're interested in being with women who are their age.

Take Marilyn's friend, Bob. He's sixty-six and kind of looks it but is vibrant and attractive and curious. He told a story about being pursued by a thirty-three-year-old woman, who would show up at his house unexpectedly when he didn't text her back. He had to explain to her at least five times that he wasn't interested. Her attention was flattering but also annoying, especially as Bob doesn't kid himself about where he is in life. "Look at me," he said. "Yes, I'm in decent shape. But I look old enough to be her father. I am old enough to be her father. What's *wrong* with her?"

And here's the difference between an MNB and a hot-drop. The hot-drop is easily seduced by the younger woman, usually a woman who wants to start the reproductive cycle with him. The MNB is at a different place in his life. He's not looking to reproduce. Nor are the women he dates.

Like Carla, fifty-four. She had a high-powered career in the city, but due to the usual vagaries of life ended up single and in the Village with her teenage son. She started her own small firm, which is flourishing. She's got it all together. Or appears to, anyway.

What Carla is looking for in a partner is defined by what she's not looking for this time around. "I'm not looking for a guy to take care of me. I'm not looking for a guy to put a roof over my head. And I'm not looking to get married." Carla's marriage was, she says, "damaging" and an experience that at this point she doesn't want to repeat. On the other hand, she doesn't want to be alone.

"I want someone to be an equal," she says. "They've got to carry their share of the load. And they've got to be there emotionally. Because what I've found in life is that shit happens to all of us, and it's just a little better if you don't have to go through it alone."

And that's the other reality about dating in middle age. Shit does happen. You are dealing with people who have not only gone through stuff but may be going through it while you're just getting to know them. Chances are, someone's going to lose a parent. Someone's going to lose a job. Someone's going to lose a friend.

In this case, I was that someone.

A Cancer Christmas Tree

My father was dying. He'd survived cancer for twenty years, but now it was back.

He called me up. He told me how he'd gone to get a scan that revealed every nook and cranny of where the cancer had spread and the results weren't good. "Candy," he said. "My body was lit up like a Christmas tree."

I went to visit him. He drove us to a restaurant, the same restaurant where we'd have the luncheon after the church and before we went to the graveyard on the day of my father's upcoming funeral. He had it all planned out and he wanted to tell me about it.

The host led us to a table next to the window. My father was joking and charming, the way he always was. I sat down stiffly and looked out the window. Across the street was the building where my mother and her best friend started their first business, a travel agency. On Wednesdays, when school got out early, I'd take the bus an extra stop and visit my mother at her office. I can still remember the smell of paper and new carpet and fresh paint and how she and her best friend were so proud to be businesswomen.

I looked back at my father, at his gnarled hand—so similar in shape and appearance to my own—and realized I wasn't sure I could do this. Talk to my father about his funeral while being in a MAM dive.

I'd recently had a series of setbacks, as my father might say. I was scared about my finances and I was scared about my future.

But I was also scared for my father to know that I was in a bad place. My father had always been proud of me. I didn't want him to die thinking that I was a failure after all.

I told him that I'd finally met someone.

I always told my father about my boyfriends. In fact, I went further and made an effort to introduce them to the poor man.

This was, on the face of it, probably not a good idea. My father prided himself on "knowing men" and most of them in his opinion were highly flawed. He had once chased one of my sister's boyfriends off the property—a suburban lawn—because he was a bad boy who only wanted one thing.

And yet, for some reason, I continued to bring boyfriends home to meet my father. Afterward, my father would shake his head. "Mama's boy," he'd said about one. "Completely selfish," he'd said about another. "Do you notice how everything is 'his' and 'mine'?" When the inevitable breakup would occur, my father always congratulated me on having gotten away from someone who wasn't quite good enough.

"Well," my father said, as I finished telling him about MNB. "He sounds like a gentleman." He paused. "Tell him that I would have loved to meet him, but I'm afraid I can't."

And so the day came. I called up MNB. "My father died," I said, and then I cried a little.

"I'm coming right over," he said.

As I waited, I realized that while I was prepared for my dad's passing, I hadn't considered the possibility of going through this sad and incredibly personal moment with a relative stranger.

MNB had never met my father or my family. What was the protocol?

"I'll be there for you however you'd like," he said. "You tell me what you need me to do and I'll do it."

I thought about what was ahead. The long drive. The three-hour viewing with an open casket. The overnight at the B&B and then the funeral and lunch and then the cemetery, where my father would be laid to rest next to my mother, my uncle, my grandmother, grandfather, and great-grandmother. And there would be the old friends, the few who were left, and a handful of relatives.

It wouldn't be fun. On the other hand, it would be nicer to have him by my side. Did I know him well enough to ask? Did I trust him enough to take the chance?

I asked anyway. "Will you come with me to the funeral?"

"I'd love to," he said.

It was that easy.

It had been a lousy autumn and the leaves were brown as we drove up to Connecticut.

"It's going to be okay," MNB said, as he squeezed my hand. "Remember, we're in this together."

And even though it was a crappy moment in life, I realized it could have been a hell of a lot worse.

I squeezed back.

"I love you," I said.

"I love you, too."

Of course, we had no idea if we actually meant it. Or what it meant if we did. Who does ever know? But maybe that's one of the good things about middle age: some things don't change.

CHAPTER NINE

THE SUPER MIDDLES

O N THE other hand, plenty of other things do change. Somewhere in the middle of the new middle age, people begin to fall into two categories: the "super middles" and "everyone else."

Everyone else is pretty easy to spot. They're like most of us who look in the mirror and do not recognize our own faces. This one degree of facial separation is one of nature's mysterious tricks, and no matter what you do, few can escape it. At the same time, there's a certain democracy about it. In the middle-aged softening, you can't really tell who was a beauty in their twenties from someone who was plain; nor can you believe that the bald guy who now looks like a potato was once a hot stud. And vice versa. He can't believe you ever had long hair and a body someone would want to see in a bikini. In this syndrome, it's common to go to parties and run into old friends whom you haven't seen for a while and who don't recognize you. Happily, you'll find yourself able to return the favor all too often.

At first, this one-degree-of-separation recognition gives life a slightly surreal edge, but one soon gets used to it. Indeed, it becomes just another middle-aged conundrum to bond over.

Scattered throughout the crowd, however, will be another category of middle-ager altogether. They "haven't aged at all" and look "exactly the same." Indeed, due to a diligent health routine and the right cosmetic touches, they may even appear to have aged backward.

Meet the "super middles." They are like they were before, but better.

Take Carl. Twenty years ago when he was living the reproductive lifestyle, Carl was a mess. He was out of shape, anxiety ridden, and he had the energy of a jack-in-the-box. Now he's confident and fit, wearing designer Italian. He's got all his hair, which helps. He drives a fast convertible and looks good doing it.

Most of Carl's once-successful friends, however, burned out. Like sensible middle-agers, they now spend their afternoons golfing and their mornings going to doctors. Not Carl. He started his own company, which requires him to spend a lot of time with cool people in their thirties.

Yes, Carl is annoying because it is annoying to have conversations about "cool thirtysomething people" whom no one older than fifty actually cares about. But still, you have to admire the guy.

And then there's Victor. He was an eight-hundred-dollar-an-hour corporate lawyer until he got divorced, got fired, hit bottom, and charged back up, realizing his true calling was to help others.

He got his pilot's license, bought a small plane, and now flies it to disaster areas in need of supplies.

Victor is a good person.

And this, indeed, is the hallmark of the super middles. They are trying to be better people, not just physically, but spiritually, psychologically, and psychically. They are about improvement and a determined happiness. This time, they're going to get things right.

Like Marilyn's new friend, Rebecca.

Ten years ago, Rebecca was one of those "I don't know how she does it" women. Then she hit fifty. Her husband lost his job, they got divorced, and then she lost her job and went through a typical MAM period, during which she filled her time drinking and engaging with inappropriate men. One night, when a guy she'd pinned her hopes on told her he was seeing two other women as well, she became enraged and slapped him across the face. He socked her in the shoulder and sent her reeling. There was a police report. Then she was caught outside the school grounds driving over the limit and that was it.

She stopped drinking and started exercising—boxing at first because she was so angry—and slowly her life started to turn around.

She's now training for a mini triathlon and has started another business helping women make investments. It's doing so well she recently bought a bigger house.

The biggest change is that she is no longer angry at herself. When she drank too much or ate too much or just in general fucked up, she would berate herself continually, and now she feels so much happier because she doesn't have to waste time being angry at herself for fucking up. Did I get it?

Yes I nodded. I did.

And because she got it, Rebecca had just found her own MNB, a super middle guy named Brad.

Like Rebecca, he was an extreme exerciser, dedicated to an hour of Qigong a day, along with waterskiing and yoga. And because he was a super middle, he wasn't afraid to express his feelings for Rebecca—he thought she might be the one—nor was he afraid of commitment.

Indeed, in true super middle style, Brad wanted to move in with her even though they'd only been seeing each other for four months.

He also wanted to introduce her to his family.

Marilyn and I were at Kitty's one afternoon when Rebecca came roaring in. Brad, being super middle perfect, had chartered a private plane to take Rebecca to a family reunion at their compound in Maine.

We all congratulated her on her extreme good luck. Exclamations of "that's wonderful" and "what are you going to wear?" echoed around the kitchen.

"But I don't want to go," Rebecca said.

She was angry he'd even asked. Thinking he was making some kind of romantic gesture, he'd sprung this outing on her out of the blue, when she already had plans for the weekend. Plans with friends that she didn't want to cancel. Plans that Brad should have remembered. Why should she cancel plans with her old friends to go hang out with strangers?

But they wouldn't exactly be strangers we pointed out. They were Brad's relatives, the implication being that they might someday be her own.

"They're still strangers," she countered.

And around and around it went, with all of the women taking the side of the "relationship" over the fact that Rebecca selfishly, we assumed, didn't want to go to Maine for the weekend. Because selfishness is not allowed, especially when a super middle man of solvent means is concerned.

And so, Rebecca went to the family reunion and she was miserable but she thought it would pass.

Two weeks later, Brad began moving his stuff in.

Marilyn and I went to a party at Rebecca's new house to celebrate Brad, the house, and the new vistas that middle age were opening up. All you had to do was to look around at the guests to believe it. Everyone was attractive and gleefully admitted to being older than they appeared. The men had biceps and the women had those tight glutes and quads that look good in exercise pants. Everyone was doing something somewhat important and meaningful with their lives and that was what counted. The room was filled with platitudes, happy clichés, and laughter.

"It's all about beautiful, healthy people coming together," Rebecca declared. "Age is irrelevant now and we're all in new territory. There are no rules. Relationships can be anything."

Except when they can't.

At some point, after Marilyn and I left the party to go home to get a good super middle's night's sleep, Brad went "crazy" and started dancing and doing his Elvis Presley imitation. Perhaps this would have been okay, but Rebecca's twenty-two-year-old daughter came home in the middle of it and declared Brad's impersonation a sight she could never unsee and ran into her room and locked the door. Rebecca tried to soothe her daughter but gave up and instead spent three hours cleaning up the party mess while Brad lay on the couch watching TV.

And while Brad was merely behaving like a typical man in a typical heterosexual relationship, Rebecca decided this wasn't okay after all.

She broke up with him the next morning.

Brad was devastated. Marilyn saw him at a meeting and he started crying when he talked about Rebecca and how much he'd cared for her. That's how sensitive and wonderful these new middle-aged men were, and Marilyn said Rebecca was a real fool to break up with him. He was a great guy and he had everything.

A couple of months later, Rebecca was dating someone else. I wondered if middle-aged dating was not going to end up being some beautiful new experience, as Rebecca had hoped, but instead just another version of the serial dating we did back in our twenties and thirties.

What would that be like?

I got some idea when a couple of super middles came to stay at Kitty's.

Like many super middles, they were in their sixties. This makes sense, considering that MAM can eat up more years than you think. By the time you get it together, you've clocked another decade. But that might be the only thing that's older about these super middles.

Kimberly, sixty-one, and Steven, sixty-seven, were a good example. Kimberly was once an actress, but she'd given it up when she had kids. Steven, who used to be an Olympic skier, was now a ski instructor in Aspen. We weren't sure what their relationship was. Steven was an old friend of Kitty's, and when he asked if he could come and stay, she said yes. She thought maybe he would turn out to be interested in her, but then he called and asked if he could bring a friend.

"Is she his girlfriend?" I asked. "Why is he bringing her?"

"I have no idea," Kitty said.

They arrived with several bags, which they put in the same room. Like so many super middles, they were obsessed with their health. After unpacking their bags, they brought down containers of special vitamins and tinctures that needed to be stored in the refrigerator.

They went back upstairs, put on their bathing suits, and went outside.

They had typical super middle bodies. Meaning, due to the ten or twelve or so hours they put into exercise every week, they were in far better shape than most people of any age. And they knew it. They were not the least bit afraid to strut around in their sixtysomething bodies clad in just small scraps of fabric.

They did that for a while and then they spotted the paddle-boards. When a super middle sees any kind of board, they're compelled to get on it. Sure enough, the two dove into the water, swam around the paddleboards, and vaulted on top. When I saw them paddling back thirty minutes later, I made Kitty go outside with me.

"I hate them," Kitty said.

"I do, too. But we have to be friendly. Otherwise we'll look like the weird ones."

When they got back to land, I tried to make conversation by asking Kimberly about how the paddle had gone. "It was beautiful. It was so Zen." She looked me up and down. "You should try it."

I smiled. I have, I wanted to say, and I didn't find it at all Zen. And neither did Kitty.

I suddenly realized that it might be difficult to communicate with these super middles. They were all about vitamins, exercises, and Zenness, a language Kitty and I didn't speak.

But then I found something Kimberly and I could talk about. She had an invention!

She wasn't the first super middle woman I'd met who'd recently invented something. One had invented a filter for a phone screen. Another had come up with a formula for a new kind of fabric. Kimberly had invented a machine that could destroy cellulite. A lot of people were clamoring for it and now she had to figure out how to manufacture the machine. She'd just gotten back from a trip to China.

On the first night at the hotel, she cried. She was afraid she couldn't do it. Afraid she was a fraud. She called her son.

"You can do it, Mom," he said. "We know you can do it. We believe in you."

She hung up and she did it. She was there for ten days. It was her company and she was working all the time, trying to get it right.

Now she finally had a free weekend and she wanted to relax.

I brought the topic around to Steven. Were they together?

The answer was complicated. Steven was still married, but he didn't live with his wife anymore, who lived in Denver. In any case, he had out of the blue asked her to come on this trip and she said yes. They were old friends from the 1980s. He was a "great guy" and she'd always "loved him as a person."

He and Kimberly came into the kitchen to take more vitamins. They talked about the benefits of B12, then suggested we all take a B12 capsule. Kitty and I passed. Kimberly told us this was probably a good idea because we could potentially be in the 5 percent of the population who're allergic to B12 and will blow up like a balloon upon taking it. Then they reassured us not to worry about them and went back up to their room.

Some time passed. Enough that Kitty and I became curious. "What kind of houseguests go up to their room in the middle of the afternoon and just stay in there?" she asked.

"Maybe they're having sex."

I went upstairs to find out.

As I crept down the hall, I heard music and giggling. Their door was open a crack, probably because it didn't quite shut unless you closed it hard.

I peeked inside. I got a split-second glance of them lying on the bed in their bathing suits laughing at some private joke they found hilariously funny before they spotted me.

"Hello?" Kimberly said.

"Come in," Steven said, sitting up.

"Yes?" Kimberly asked.

"Um," I said. It was summer, so I asked the obvious question: "Do you want some corn?"

"Corn?" Kimberly said. She looked at Steven. "I'm so fucking sick of corn. No, I don't want any more corn." And then they both laughed.

"What are you, the hall monitor?" Steven said, which made them laugh even harder.

I felt like the teenage geek who's just stumbled upon the head cheerleader and the quarterback making out. As I took refuge in the kitchen, I wondered if middle-aged dating was going to end up being just like high school.

Was this cycle of mate selection and rejection going to go on forever?

Later I asked Queenie: "If you and your boyfriend broke up, would you try to find someone else?"

"Oh yes," she said.

"What about if you were sixty?"

"Uh-huh."

"*Seventy?*"

"Of course."

"Eighty?"

"Why not?" Queenie brought up a mutual friend who was eighty-three and had recently found a new boyfriend.

And indeed, why not. In middle-aged dating and beyond, people aren't partnering up to get a life. They already have a life—children and exes and parents and work—so this time around, a relationship is about enhancing your life. It reminded me of the relationship theory we'd spout to ourselves back in our twenties and thirties: a relationship should be the icing on the cake of your life, not your *life*.

And now, apparently, this was possible.

"What about you?" Queenie asked. "If you and your MNB broke up, would you try to find someone else?"

I didn't know the answer to that question. But Marilyn did.

✳   ✳   ✳

Marilyn had decided that she and her MNB were going to get married. He hadn't asked her yet, but she knew he was going to, very soon. They were going on vacation in Italy and he had a jeweler friend there and said he wanted to buy her a ring.

And in the time-honored way in the world of women, Marilyn already had the wedding planned out.

They'd get married on the beach where they loved to walk. Then they'd go to the nearby miniature golf course for the wedding meal. The clubhouse had a small, old-timey restaurant that served breakfast all day, so the wedding guests could have a feast of pancakes and bacon, waffles, sausages, real maple syrup, French toast, and several types of eggs benedict served with a thick hollandaise sauce.

We would all be bridesmaids I was sure. Me, Sassy, Kitty, and probably half a dozen other women—Marilyn had a large network of girlfriends—all of whom adored her and would do anything for her. I suggested that we walk from the beach to the miniature golf course. It was only about a mile and a half, and that way we'd get in twenty minutes of exercise to mediate the thousands of calories we would consume at the wedding breakfast.

Sassy wondered if we should all wear hats. She was going to wear a hat and she wasn't going to walk.

Kitty didn't want to walk either and had already decided she wasn't going to eat any of the breakfast and would only have coffee. We wondered if the whole bridesmaids thing was silly. Then we decided we should do what we wanted. Why should we care what other people thought?

Marilyn said she wanted someone to scatter rose petals on the beach.

The very idea of Marilyn's wedding felt like a triumph. Of the possible over the impossible. Of the moving forward against decline. Of personality and passion and belief over age and MAM and whatever else life throws at you.

Marilyn's getting married felt like proof that every once in a while, just like in a movie, a person can get their happy ending. And of all the women we knew, it felt like Marilyn deserved hers the most.

But life just doesn't work that way.

CHAPTER TEN

MIDDLE-AGED SADNESS: MARILYN'S STORY

T HE YEAR before, at the end of that MAM winter when we'd all been scared about our futures,
Marilyn took these fears one step further and
slit her wrists. Although she slit them vertically and not
horizontally—a difference she'd looked up on the internet
she would explain later—Marilyn did not die. Instead she
bled for two hours and then got in her car and drove herself
the half mile to the walk-in clinic. She was swiftly trans-
ported to Southampton Hospital, from which she was able
to make a few quick phone calls before being transferred
to the state clinic mid-island.

Every couple of days I'd get a phone call from her and she'd
tell me about it. It was grim. No matter what happened she
said, she was never, ever going back there again.

They finally let her out ten days later. Marilyn's brother

241

flew in from Australia to take Marilyn back to Sydney. And it was there that Marilyn finally got the right diagnosis: she was bipolar.

It made sense. Her father was bipolar as well. Even so, Marilyn resisted the diagnosis at first. She told me she cried when the doctor told her. She couldn't accept it. She didn't want to be a bipolar person. She was ashamed.

But the doctor explained it was really just a disease, like diabetes. Lots of people had diabetes and they managed it by taking medication.

Marilyn vowed to change her life. She stopped drinking, and she exercised every day. She saw her shrink regularly and looked better than she had in years.

And she fixed up her house. It was now pristine, a pretty white house that sat straight up on top of a small hill, with a violet-colored front door. Violets being her favorite flowers, and "Violet" being the name of both her grandmother and her former dog.

Her gardens were in bloom. Marilyn had been working on them for three years, including a year of mulching. At the beginning, I'd gone with her to the gardening classes she attended every Sunday morning at ten like a regular churchgoer. I abandoned them after fidgeting through a sixty-minute lecture about the right way to water plants. But Marilyn kept at it, and now her hard work was paying off. She and her house had come a long way.

And once again, we could talk. Especially about that MAM

summer when we'd had the terrible altercation. She hadn't realized it, but she was manic at the time.

Was she sure about getting married? I asked. Why, when she didn't have to?

"Because I've finally found him," she said. "My man."

Marilyn and her MNB went to Italy and Marilyn came back with a gold ring with two diamonds, although she insisted that technically they weren't officially engaged. And then three months passed. Three months in which Marilyn seemed more than happy. Indeed, everyone said she was better than ever. She was working and she was very, very fit. She would stare adoringly at her MNB at the parties and dinners we sometimes attended now as a foursome with my MNB.

And then, as usually happens with the addition of a relationship, Marilyn and I didn't see each other as much as we used to. None of us did. Marilyn was busy. She was planning to airbnb her house during summer weekends and spent all her spare time organizing her belongings to get it ready.

It wasn't until two weeks after Memorial Day that Kitty, Sassy, and I compared notes and realized that none of us had actually talked to Marilyn for a few days. I thought I had the answer: Marilyn was sick. The day before, she had canceled on a girls' lunch at the last minute, claiming she wasn't feeling well.

Now we tried calling her to no avail. A couple of minutes later, we got a text. Her health insurance was canceled and did we know of a good insurance company?

Insurance issues weren't unusual for Marilyn. Over the years, as a single woman with her own business, with financial ups and downs, and with a variety of small medical issues, Marilyn occasionally had these battles. Sassy texted her a few recommendations.

Another day went by. Marilyn texted Sassy that her MNB was going to help her figure out her insurance and not to worry after all.

We were worried. But unlike in the past when she'd had difficult days, this time Marilyn wasn't alone in her house. She was staying with her MNB.

I knew this for a fact because her car was parked at his place. I passed by every day on my way to the beach, the same beach where Marilyn was hoping to get married.

That Saturday, when I saw her car, I thought about stopping in. But then I didn't want to bother her. It would be rude to go barging in on her when she was at her boyfriend's house.

Late Sunday afternoon, when I passed the house again, I noticed that Marilyn's car wasn't there. I assumed this meant the renters had vacated and Marilyn had gone back to her place.

I called her, but it went to voice mail.

When I went to bed, I tried her again. Her mailbox was full. This was strange. Marilyn always checked her messages. I decided to stop by her house the next morning.

I never got there. I was prevented by a strange set of circumstances that I still can't explain to this day.

I woke late and decided to run some errands in town and then because it was a beautiful day to bike over to Marilyn's house.

I wrote out some checks for bills, placed stamps on the envelopes, and stowed them in the zippered bike pouch along with my wallet and cell phone.

My first stop was the bank. I plucked my wallet out of the bike pouch, went into the bank, and stuck my card in the ATM.

Immediately there was a problem.

"Transaction denied."

I felt a sense of foreboding.

"What the hell?" I stomped over to a teller. "There's something wrong with my card."

A sigh. "It's probably the machine."

It wasn't. We tried all the machines and then the people in the bank tried their computers and still couldn't figure out what was wrong, so they did the transactions by hand.

I left the bank not at all reassured. On my way out, a young man called my name. "Hey, Candace. How are you?"

"Fine?" I said, flustered. Who was this guy and how did he know me?

"I recognized your bike outside."

Ah, right, the guy from the bike shop. "It's a beautiful day for a ride," he said.

"Yes, it is," I replied.

My mood lifted. I reminded myself that the bank incident was but one small glitch in what would undoubtedly be a good day. I'd head to the post office next, then over to Marilyn's.

But as I approached my bike, I noticed that something else was wrong. The bike pouch was unzipped.

I hadn't left it like that, had I? If I had, that would be unusual. But perhaps I hadn't been paying attention. I opened the flap and gasped.

It was empty—or at least the bills were gone. My cell phone was still there.

Had I been robbed? If so, why hadn't they taken my cell phone?

I approached a young traffic cop, ruddy faced and barely an adult, who was standing in the crosswalk.

"Excuse me," I said. "Did you see anyone lingering around that orange bike over there?"

He glanced over. "No."

"Are you sure?"

"Yes."

"Because I think I've been robbed."

That got his attention. He strolled over, grasping the intercom on his shoulder and bringing it closer to his mouth, as if ready to report the crime. "What'd they take?" he asked.

"Some mail."

"Mail?"

"Bills."

He put down the walkie-talkie. "Why would anyone take someone's bills?"

I struggled to explain. "They weren't really bills. They were checks. You know. When you pay bills? They had stamps on them."

"Why would anyone take that?"

I could see how I looked to him: a confused middle-aged woman with frazzled hair and a neon green safety vest on an orange bike insisting that someone stole her bills.

I don't think so.

"Maybe I forgot them at my house," I whispered as I edged away.

I got back on the bike. Panting my way towards home, I went over this strange series of events again and again. They felt connected by a force field of unstable, chaotic energy. And with a plunge, I realized I'd had this feeling before—on the day that Tucco died.

I got to my house, threw down my bike and checked my phone. I'd gotten a call from Stacey, one of Marilyn's Miami friends.

For a second I thought, Why is Stacey calling me?

And then I knew.

Marilyn took her life sometime late Sunday night or early Monday morning.

She left no note, but she did leave a will.

She wanted to be cremated.

And that was it. No ceremony. No nothing. Just a box full of gritty ashes.

At first, some of Marilyn's close friends and family from out of town rushed in and there was a poignant and naturally awkward memorial, but then they left and it was just Sassy and Kitty and me and sometimes Queenie. We felt Marilyn's loss everywhere and especially in the day-to-day. As Kitty said, she couldn't believe that Marilyn wasn't going to come walking through the door at any second, her laptop computer under her arm and the large leather sack containing her purse and files slung over her shoulder. Marilyn had moved to the country but a part of her would always be a schlepper.

We felt encased in our grief, trapped under a perpetual low-hanging cloud. We couldn't move. We couldn't breathe. We were exhausted. We'd go to each other's houses and sit at the kitchen table and stare.

We'd ask why.

We pointed out that she was in love and about to get married. That she and her MNB would have had a great life together. She was doing so well. Feeling so good. Maybe she was feeling too good and she'd stopped taking her medication? It was the only explanation we could come up with.

There had been a spate of deaths and suicides that month. Mostly women in their fifties, women like Marilyn who'd appeared to have had it all. Like everyone else, they didn't. Lurking in the background were financial issues or relationship issues or health issues. But mostly, what you sensed was the fear. The pure terror of the unknown future.

The fear that you were a failure. That no one would love you ever or again. That you were truly alone. That no one cared and it was only going to get worse. That there was no imaginary bright future to hide behind when it came to the truth.

These were the fears that crept into our bones like the cold, damp weather during that long winter. And so we worried. About ourselves and each other. When you're a single, child-free woman like Marilyn, the world wonders what's going to happen to you, and so you wonder yourself. As a single, child-free woman, there really is no script for you.

Time passed, and though we no longer talked about Marilyn every day I couldn't stop thinking about her. When I went to the beach, I'd drive by the house of her MNB, and I'd remember that last weekend and wonder what she'd been doing.

Sometimes my route would take me by Marilyn's house. This was always startling. Her small white car was still in the driveway, parked where it always had been, and it was impossible not to imagine that Marilyn herself was inside the house, perched on one of the couches across from the large coffee table where she did her work on her laptop while fielding calls.

And sometimes I'd pretend that Marilyn was still here. I'd tell myself that she went away for a couple of months and she'll be back soon and I'd think about all the things I'd tell her. Like the news that MNB and I are still together. And that Tilda Tia has given up dating and is only going to concentrate on her career but still has hopes of a picket fence love someday. And mostly that Sassy bought a new house on our favorite street in the Village. It has a view, and it's right across the water from Kitty's house. There's been lots of talk about paddle-board parties that we both know will never happen because Sassy hates wearing bathing suits and Kitty refuses to exercise.

And then the day came when I passed by Marilyn's house and her car was gone.

And that, I thought sadly, was that.

Except it wasn't.

Sassy and I had some of Marilyn's ashes.

Marilyn's brother had given her MNB her ashes and her MNB had given some of them to us. They were in stacked, clear plastic containers that Marilyn, an ace organizer, had given to him just before she'd died, back when she was cleaning things up to airbnb her house. "Here," she'd said to him. "You might need these someday."

Now the containers with the ashes were resting in a large, silver-plated urn in the front parlor of Sassy's house. The ashes themselves were dark gray and flecked with white grit that might have been bone. Sassy had to pass by them every day.

At least once a week, she'd call me up. "We've got to do it," she'd say.

And so, on what Sassy called a navy-blue day at the end of September, the kind of day on which Marilyn had hoped to get married, instead of scattering rose petals, we would scatter her ashes.

Or at least we thought we would.

Tilda Tia came and stayed with me. She said, "How are you?" And I said, "I'm doing fine," even though Marilyn's was the second major death, including my dad's, that I'd had in six months.

Of course, I wasn't the only one. Two months ago Tilda Tia had lost one of her childhood friends to cancer. She'd been there when it happened and had held her friend's hand.

We hugged.

And that's one of the things you learn from MAM. How to accept loss and keep going.

We walked over to Sassy's new house, where we met up with Kitty, who had just learned she was going to become a grandmother, and Queenie, whose daughter had gone off to college.

We talked about how great it would have been if Marilyn were there with us. How she would have loved seeing all her friends together. How, partly thanks to her, we'd all ended up in the same place.

And then we walked to the end of the dock on the bay where Marilyn had first landed in the Village just three years ago.

Sassy and I each carried a container of the ashes. The idea was that we would open them and everyone would take a handful and when the ashes were scattered, we would light sparklers.

Immediately, there was a glitch. The ridges in the tops of the containers were embedded with the dust of Marilyn's ashes and were stuck. No amount of gentle prying was going to get them loose.

For a moment we stood there, wondering what to do. This, we agreed, was very Marilyn. As Sassy said, she'd always had a stubborn side. She'd usually do the opposite of what everyone told her to do. A trait, frankly, that could be applied to all of us, in this group anyway.

"It's a sign," Queenie said. "She doesn't want to go."

And so we brought Marilyn's ashes back into the house.

I was relieved. There was something about the ash scattering that didn't sit right with me.

The week before, I'd run into Marilyn's MNB on the beach. He'd just gotten the toxicology report and it turned out that Marilyn had been taking the proper medications all along.

In short, she'd done everything right, and somehow it still wasn't enough. We'll never understand the reason for her death.

But that wasn't the only mystery. There was the disappearance of those bills on the day she died. Someone mailed them and it wasn't me, because days after Marilyn's death, I was getting angry calls from creditors over the checks I'd had to cancel.

I couldn't help but wonder if somehow Marilyn—or her spirit anyway—was involved.

And as we gathered once again around the kitchen table, I realized we did know one thing.

Now, more than ever, we had to be there for each other. And we would be.

The End

Epilogue

Happily Ever After After All?

The inevitable happened. Time passed. And suddenly it was almost a year and a half that MNB and I had been dating. Somewhere along the way, we'd entered coupledom.

We didn't technically live together, but we knew one another's patterns and did couple things, like going out with other couples and traveling together and creating a family adjacent scenario in which my two dogs, Pepper and Prancer, were sort of our kids. But mostly we'd developed a routine that worked. A way of being around each other in the same space. Because what is a relationship really but two bodies orbiting each other in space and time?

And like planets, it's hard to resist the pull of partnering. Once you enter into the relationship phase it's like being inside one of those Russian dolls or Dante's Inferno or maybe just Mario Brothers—you reach one level and you just have to try to get to the next. In other words, for the first time, after nearly a year and a half together, I found myself asking, what if MNB and I got married and he became MNH?

I didn't know why I was asking the question. It wasn't that I couldn't see myself growing old with MNB in some vague and fuzzy future, but at this moment, irl, it would only make our lives much more complicated.

And yet, there was something about later-life marriage that was in the air. These days, when people ask what I'm writing about and I tell them, they all have a story. It's a story, they promise, that will be unlike anything I've ever heard before.

"Try me," I say.

Then they tell me a convoluted tale about two people who suddenly find themselves single and finally, after all these years, discover each other (usually again) and fall in love and get married and have a wedding with a hundred of their friends. And there is nothing new about this story except for the age of the participants. They are always over seventy. Sometimes they are eighty-three. Sometimes they are ninety-four. In any case, when these weddings happen they're apparently really beautiful because what is more beautiful than showing the world that true love does work in the end. And everyone cries.

Then the wedding bug hit Tilda Tia.

She called me up. "You won't believe what's happened," she said.

I already knew what had happened from Kitty and Queenie. As of one month ago, Tilda Tia had a new boyfriend and he was a real MNB. He had a two-bedroom apartment on the Upper West Side and a regular job in finance, and, since he was a really nice guy, he was helping Tilda Tia move into her new apartment.

"I met someone," she announced.

"I heard," I said.

"No, but I mean, I met *someone*. I mean, I would not be surprised if I have a ring on my finger by this time next year."

"Really?"

"Seriously. And when I say ring, I mean my wedding ring. My engagement ring I'll probably get in six months."

"So you'll be married in a year?" I said.

"Yes. Why not?" she said.

"Are you going to have a wedding?"

"Of course I'm going to have a wedding," she said. "What is wrong with you?"

"And bridesmaids?"

"Yes. And they are all going to match," she said.

I tried to envision this phenomenon of middle-aged people getting married with all the fixings. Like dance floors and eighties music. With some super middle spinning around on his back in a long-forgotten break-dancing move. Getting teary-eyed over "St. Elmo's Fire" and pointing fingers at each other as everyone boogied. Sure, it was embarrassing. But if you didn't care, it could be fun.

"Hello?" Tilda Tia said. "Are you there?"

"Are you going to play Michael Jackson?" I asked. "And what about 'St. Elmo's Fire'?"

"'St. Elmo's Fire'? What is wrong with you?" Tilda Tia asked. "By the way, Kitty and I are wondering what you're going to do for your birthday."

My birthday. I groaned.

"It's a big one, isn't it?"

"Mmmhmm."

"Are you going to tell people your age? Because I wouldn't if I were you. You could just keep saying you're fifty-nine. I know four women who did that through their late sixties. And who cares? After a certain age, no one pays that much attention."

This, I had to agree, was true.

One of the things about fiftysomething birthdays is that people tend to forget them. Once you pass the big five-oh, they're not that significant. Partly because at a certain point, you realize there's not that much of a difference between fifty-eight and fifty-two. And partly because after fifty, it's easy to somehow lose track of your age and not remember whether you are fifty-two, fifty-five, or fifty-eight, as happened to Kitty a couple of months ago. It turned out she was fifty-five, which to Kitty was such a "nothing" number that she actually forgot it was even her birthday. I could also recall a couple of birthdays in the last decade where I'd been content to just raise a glass of champers to myself and call it a day.

But then I'd met MNB. MNB was a lot of things, but mostly he was an organizer guy. And so, three months before the big six-oh, MNB began asking questions. What did I want to do to celebrate? Did I want to fly to London and have dinner at a nightclub? Or maybe go someplace warm for the weekend? All of which sounded wonderful, but would also require extra helpings of effort. There would be packing and then getting to the airport and waiting in line at security and then possibly at customs and I realized that while I was often willing to do these things for others, the one person I wasn't willing to do it for was myself. And especially not for my birthday.

Plus, I hate "decade" birthdays the way I hate New Year's Eve. Somehow, they're supposed to be more fun than any other party, when in reality the best times are always the parties that aren't planned, when things just happen.

And sure enough, when I think back on decade birthdays, with the exception of thirty, both forty and fifty were a bit of a bummer. I'd been dumped a week before my fortieth by a guy I'd dated for six months. He said, "I'm breaking up with you because you're turning forty and you're totally neurotic about it and I can't deal." Even though I thought I was handling it really well. Still, on the morning of my birthday when my mother called, I started crying. "I'm forty. And I'm not married and I never will be."

"Please don't make a big deal out of it," my mother said. "Age is not that important."

And she was right, because lots of great things happened in my forties. I did get married. I worked a lot. I made a home. And for some reason, I thought it would go on forever.

What it did was grind on, because by the time fifty came along, all I remember was that I was tired. So very, very tired. I had a recurring dream that I was in an office building on my way to a meeting and I collapsed in front of the elevators and I just lay there and could not get up.

And now another decade has passed. And, as it has been for so many others, it was a decade of change. Of moving, divorce, and death. Of rediscovering old friendships and finding new ways to have relationships. People in their fifties have to be like little engines that could, restarting themselves again and again until something kicks in, turns over, and there you are on the track once more.

And it's okay. Because who would have thought that turning sixty feels a bit like waking up from a bad dream?

Maybe it was time to have a party after all. Even just a small one. And no, I wasn't going to lie about my age. Fifty-nine forever?

I don't think so.

And so as Kitty, Queenie, Sassy, Tilda Tia, my MNB, and I gathered at Omar's, we raised a glass to all that had passed and all we hoped was to come. And looking around I knew one thing. Sixty had arrived and it was going to be fabulous.

ACKNOWLEDGMENTS

Thank you to Morgan Entrekin, Elisabeth Schmitz, Judy Hottensen, Katie Raissian, Deb Seager, Justina Batchelor, Gretchen Mergenthaler, Julia Berner-Tobin, and the rest of the terrific team at Grove Atlantic. Thanks also to Nicole Dewey and, as always, to Heather Schroder.